Preparing Room

Preparing Room

An Advent Companion

Russell J. Levenson Jr.

CHURCH
PUBLISHING
INCORPORATED

A version of this book was previously published by Insight Press.

Church Publishing
19 East 34th Street
New York, NY 10016
www.churchpublishing.org

Cover art: *Falling Graces* by Russell J. Levenson Jr.
Cover design by Jennifer Kopec, 2Pug Design
Typesetting by Denise Hoff

A record of this book is available from the Library of Congress.

ISBN-13: 978-1-64065-315-3 (paperback)
ISBN-13: 978-1-64065-316-0 (ebook)

Dedicated to those Mothers who have generously served as
God Bearers to me;
My Grandmother, Kathryn Brackin

Dear mothers who mentored me during my teen years,
Alice Jeter Kieran, Sherry Gray Thompson,
and Phyllis Walton
My wonderful Jewish Aunt, Johanna Levenson Fitzpatrick
My spiritual Mother and Dear Friend, Ann Claypool Beard
My Mother-in-Law, Evelyn Boehms Norton
My Mother, Lynne Whitney Levenson
My Daughter, Evie
And Laura,
My bride, and the love and joy of my life

Contents

Preface • In the Beginning   ix

Meditations

1 • Generators and Generations   1

2 • Trash and Treasure   6

3 • The Best-Laid Plans   10

4 • Meet and Greet   14

5 • Troubles, Fears, and Wonders   18

6 • The Only Thing to Fear . . .   21

7 • And Now . . .   24

8 • Remember Jesus   28

9 • Good News   32

10 • Bad News   35

11 • Power Play   38

12 • Facing the Scars   41

13 • U-Turn   45

14 • What's in a Name?   49

15 • Fill Her Up!   52

16 • An Act of Balance   55

17 • Impossible Possibles   59

18 • Let It Be . . .   64

19 • Relatively Speaking   67

20 • Magnifying Glass   71

21 • Circumstantial Evidence   75

22 • Smelly Truths   79

23 • Room or No Room . . . That Is the Question   83

24 • God's Angle on Shepherds   86

25 • Signs   89

26 • Treasure Chest   93

27 • Wisdom of the Ages   97

28 • Something Wicked This Way Comes   101

29 • Star Power   105

30 • Gold, Frankenstein, and Mud   110

31 • Pointing the Way   115

Afterword • Let Every Heart Prepare Him Room   119

Acknowledgments   123

Scriptural Index   125

Index of Authors Cited   129

Preface: In the Beginning

In the beginning was the Word, and the Word was
with God, and the Word was God. He was in the
beginning with God. All things came into being
through him, and without him not one thing came
into being. What has come into being in him was
life, and the life was the light of all people. The light
shines in the darkness, and the darkness did not
overcome it.

—John 1:1–5

Every story has a beginning. For those of us who walk within the
Judeo-Christian tradition, the story begins, well, in the beginning!
Unlike some families, I can only trace my lineage back a few generations. My bloodline is an amalgamation of cultures that came
together through the gifts of love and marriage. Looking at my
family tree, one would find Scottish-Irish, English, Russian, and
Native American (Creek); my religious lineage is both Christian
and Jewish. I have spent a great deal of time with the patriarchs
and matriarchs of my family seeking "the beginning" of my family's story, attempting to deal with the places and people from
whence I came.

When the story of our faith flips from the Hebrew scripture
to the gospels, we are more formally introduced to a new person
in the Trinity: Jesus. I suggest formally because as the scripture
above suggests, He was with God even in the beginning. A quick
read of Genesis and we see that when God created humankind,
God said, "Let us make humankind in our image, according to
our likeness . . . ."[1] Note the plural; God was not in it alone.

---

1 Genesis 1:26.

Advent is the season where we turn once again to the beginning of the Christian story as it centers on Jesus. The term "Advent" actually means "coming." The Advent season is the time we turn to the coming of God in the flesh in the Christ Child.

My grandmother and her mother were makers of quilts. I have inherited several of them from both. I remember as a child, coming into my great-grandmother's kitchen and seeing a quilt frame suspended from the ceiling. She was a host of what was then known as a quilting party. Several women would gather at her home, each bringing various pieces of cloth of different shades and textures. By using the frame and working together, they produced a beautiful quilt that served as a source of comfort and warmth.

The pieces of the beginning of the Christian story come together not from one set of hands, but many—combining different shades and textures. In the gospels, Mark makes no mention of the events leading up to and surrounding the birth of Jesus. John, for the most part, points back to Genesis. The birth narratives come to us from Matthew and Luke.

It may help you to know that Matthew was concerned that his readers saw Jesus as the fulfillment of the Jewish prophecies of the coming Messiah. He makes more references and uses more quotes from the Hebrew Bible than any other New Testament writer. Luke, tradition tells us, was not only a physician but also very keen on history. Getting the details correct, like any historian, was very important to him.

In the pages that follow, I hope to offer several gifts. First are the scriptures key to telling the story, which will come primarily from Matthew and Luke. I will also make allusions and references to other scriptures, all of which will offer the background for the second gift.

Once you have had a chance to reflect prayerfully on the scripture, I will offer a brief meditation. My hope is that the meditation will help you step deeper into the Advent story to see how it may, in fact, have some kind of practical and personal implication in your own life.

I will then offer a third gift: a suggestion under the heading that shares the title of this book, *Preparing Room*. Sometime between his birth in 1674 and death in 1748, the great hymnist Isaac Watts penned:

> Joy to the world! The Lord is come
> let earth receive her King;
> let every heart prepare him room[2]

Ah, how full the modern heart is today. There are so many ways to cram it full with e-mail, text messages, faxes, television, and satellite radio. Filling it even more are our worries and frets, bills and debts, health and hopes; need I go on? In hearts so full, it is sometimes difficult to place yet one more thing, thought, or feeling. Thus, each chapter will offer a reflection or suggestion on how we may prepare just a bit more room for the King.

Finally, I will share a fourth gift—a prayer from our Judeo-Christian tradition or one from my own pen.

This four-part compilation is designed to carry us through the season of Advent, beginning with the first Sunday of Advent and ending with Christmas Day. Since the Advent season varies in

---

2 *The Hymnal* (New York: The Church Hymnal Corporation, 1982), 100.

length from year to year, I have not set a corresponding day for each offering. Start as you enter the Advent season and track it along so that you end around the time of Christmas Day.

One more thing—an important piece of our quilt. Part of this work came together while I was on a study leave in London, so you will find some references to life on the other side of the pond. I got back home on a transatlantic flight. I know absolutely nothing about the mechanics of, or the techniques it takes to fly, an airliner. Once I board, I buckle my belt and say my prayers (which I always do), then I put my trust in the pilots to get me to my destination. Once we are in the air, I do not have to know the specifics about pitch and roll, rudder and wing to enjoy the ride.

There are parts of the Advent/Christmas story that may tend to get us sidetracked a bit. The modern mind may find it hard to grasp the miraculous pieces of the quilt we find in the immaculate conception, the virgin birth, the angels, signs, stars, shepherds, and magi. But if we, as passengers, spend too much time focusing on how the jetliner works, we may never simply enjoy the ride.

Do not get me wrong; there is a time to study the how. I have to trust the one flying does know how! But to get to settle into the ride, my mind and heart needs to let the pilot control the direction, so I can just enjoy the flight. May I encourage you to do the same as we move ahead? There is certainly a time for inquiry and critique of the story, but my offering here is to simply let the story speak to us. Accept it and go along for the ride, at least for this season.

And now, my friend, I invite you to open your heart, to make room for the God of us all. Let us begin, at the beginning!

—RJL+

Generators and Generations

An account of the genealogy of Jesus the Messiah, the son of David, the son of Abraham.

Abraham was the father of Isaac, and Isaac the father of Jacob, and Jacob the father of Judah and his brothers, and Judah the father of Perez and Zerah by Tamar, and Perez the father of Hezron, and Hezron the father of Aram, and Aram the father of Aminadab, and Aminadab the father of Nahshon, and Nahshon the father of Salmon, and Salmon the father of Boaz by Rahab, and Boaz the father of Obed by Ruth, and Obed the father of Jesse, and Jesse the father of King David.

And David was the father of Solomon by the wife of Uriah, and Solomon the father of Rehoboam, and Rehoboam the father of Abijah, and Abijah the father of Asaph, and Asaph the father of Jehoshaphat, and Jehoshaphat the father of Joram, and Joram the father of Uzziah, and Uzziah the father of Jotham, and Jotham the father of Ahaz, and Ahaz the father of Hezekiah, and Hezekiah the father of Manasseh, and Manasseh the father of Amos, and Amos the father of Josiah, and Josiah the father of Jechoniah and his brothers, at the time of the deportation to Babylon.

And after the deportation to Babylon: Jechoniah was the father of Salathiel, and Salathiel the father of Zerubbabel, and Zerubbabel the father of Abiud, and Abiud the father of Eliakim, and Eliakim the father of Azor, and Azor the father of Zadok, and Zadok the father of Achim, and Achim the father of Eliud, and Eliud the father of Eleazar, and Eleazar the father of

Matthan, and Matthan the father of Jacob, and Jacob the father of Joseph the husband of Mary, of whom Jesus was born, who is called the Messiah.

So all the generations from Abraham to David are fourteen generations; and from David to the deportation to Babylon, fourteen generations; and from the deportation to Babylon to the Messiah, fourteen generations.

—Matthew 1:1–17

For nearly a third of my adult life, I have lived on or near the Gulf Coast, which has its blessings and curses. On the curse side comes a little word with which few of us want familiarity: *hurricane*. I have seen and lived through my fair share. On more than one occasion, the furious winds left in their wake long power outages, made easier by an obnoxiously loud gasoline-powered generator. I did not like everything about the generator, but it kept the important things in my home going: the refrigerator, a small air conditioner, and a small radio or television to maintain contact with the outside world, at times for up to half a month. Over the years the generator has traveled with us and become part of every hurricane story we have ever told in my household.

Matthew opens our story with a genealogy of Jesus[1]—the generator of the story of Jesus. It is part of what keeps the story running and it generates the pieces that will follow. You can trace Jesus all the way back to Abraham, the adopted father of Jews, Muslims, and Christians alike. Now who would not be happy to claim Abraham as their "great, great, great, grandfather"? My own family name (Levenson) finds its roots in my great-grandfather, a Jew who immigrated to the United States in the late 1800s to escape the pogroms of Russia, a soon-to-be Communist nation. Levenson literally means "son of Levi," the ancient tribe of Israel

---

1 Luke 3:23–38; Ruth 4:18–22; 1 Chronicles 3:10–17.

given the priestly responsibility for the Ark of the Covenant and the Temple. It did not take long for me to get what we in my home call "the big head."

One of the things that really strengthens my allegiance to the story, as it is told in Holy Scripture, is its down and dirty honesty. In Jesus's family tree we find a prostitute named Rahab.[2] A snippet later, up pops King David.[3] Although much good can be said about David, he also wore the name adulterer and murderer.[4] Next comes wise King Solomon, who had more wives than most men my age have hairs on our heads. How honest though, is it not? All of these and more generate the coming of the Christ Child.

I have known many people over the years who take great pride in their lineage. I recently attended a party where a toast was given noting that their first family members came to the America on the *Mayflower*. Most would see that as something in which to have personal pride. However, it is possible to make a *religion*, perhaps even an *obsession* of sorts, about one's elders—the name, the heritage, the race—instead of seeing it as a small part of the epic story of the human family.

Perhaps more division, harm, violence, and war has been the fruit of such obsession than any other poisoned fruit of the human spirit. I recently read an article in an Irish newspaper about the lingering tensions between the United Kingdom and Northern Ireland. I grew up in the South where the color of one's skin and—in my case—hints of a name that bore Semitic roots were sources of blatant bigotry and prejudice, and continue to be in some circles.

Matthew's honesty about Jesus's generations gives us an opportunity to remember that the human beings that stepped out of the primordial dust and mud were the ancient grandparents of us all.[5]

---

2 Matthew 1:5; Joshua 2:6; Hebrews 11:31; James 2:25.

3 Matthew 1:6–7.

4 2 Samuel 12.

5 Interestingly, both the basic theories of evolution and creation share this belief that humankind came into being via the pathway of mud and air, earth and time. The pure evolutionist's *Big Bang* would be my God's breath; Genesis 2:7.

They were, like it or not, our generators. Perhaps this is why, when the Apostles began preaching the Gospel of Christ, they placed great emphasis on breaking down barriers of division. Paul wrote, "You are all children of God through faith. As many of you as were baptized into Christ have clothed yourself with Christ. There is no longer Jew or Greek, there is no longer slave or free, there is no longer male and female; for all of you are one in Christ Jesus" (Galatians 3:26–28).

How good of Matthew to include *everyone* in Jesus's family tree—even the black sheep. Perhaps it was one way of saying that it did not matter who Jesus's people were; the more important point was what the story was all about. It was generated as far back as Abraham and now, embracing it all, the curtain was about to be raised on the most important chapter.

— *Preparing Room* —

Spend some time being boldly honest about your own family tree. Are there skeletons hidden, black sheep you wish were not pasturing in your family's name? What generates your family's history and the generations before you? Does your own allegiance to your family, your race, your lifestyle, your faith cause you to lock others out of your world? Is there a chamber in your heart which needs to be swept clean of bigotry or prejudice so that it can make room for the love God wants you to shower on others?

A Prayer

Almighty God,
As you breathed your Spirit into the dust of
  the earth to give your children birth,
Breathe on me now . . .
Make eyes that are blind to the pain others see,
Make ears that hear no cry for help to hear,
Make a heart that may build walls around
  the compassion you call out of us,
Crumble into pieces, and pour out your love
  upon all you send our way.
Amen.[6]

---

6 Prayers without a citation are written by the author.

Trash and Treasure

Since many have undertaken to set down an
orderly account of the events that have been
fulfilled among us, just as they were handed on
to us by those who from the beginning were
eyewitnesses and servants of the word, I too
decided, after investigating everything carefully
from the very first, to write an orderly account for
you, most excellent Theophilus, so that you may
know the truth concerning the things about which
you have been instructed.

—Luke 1:1–4

In my business, it is not unusual to encounter the well-known
fundraising technique known as the garage sale. The church
usually issues an open invitation for folks to open their attics
and garages and unload the huge amalgamation of clothes,
toys, yard implements, framed photos, and the like. I have been
part of the sorting parties that take place prior to the big sale,
and one of the tasks is properly pricing the items. Some prices
are designed to draw customers in, while others are set just to
keep them from running the other direction. Some of what
lands in the hands of the volunteer salesperson is trash, some
is treasure.

Luke is concerned with separating things as well: fact from fiction, truth from myth. He tells his reader that he knows lots of

other people are out there trying to put the story right.[7] "Many have undertaken," he writes. I would venture to say that getting the Advent/Christmas story *right* may be difficult for many a modern mind for two reasons.

The first is the multitude of versions we now have available to us as post-millennial adults. Movies, books, television, and music all have their own versions of the story. Charles Schultz tells it well in *A Charlie Brown Christmas* when he pulls Linus on the stage to tell everyone a basic piece of the story, not through his own eyes, but through the lens of Luke's "orderly account."

We have dressed the whole story up, something which I intend, for reasons that will become obvious, to undress a bit. We have visions of a hallowed and halo-wearing Mary in a gentle and beautiful setting, with animals looking on almost knowingly, surrounded by shepherds and three wise men—all on the same night. As we will see, the story did not quite play out that way. Part of Luke's work is to set the record straight. May I suggest you let him do that for us.

The second reason it can be difficult to get the Advent/Christmas story right may be the competing voices out there. The Church has traditionally seen the season of Advent as a time in which Christians prepare for the coming of the Christ Child. The emphasis is on longing, expectation, and hope; it is also preparation that acknowledges human sin, doubt, and the darkness of the world that makes it difficult for the Christ Child to make his way into our lives.

Given the modern take on the weeks leading up to Christmas, it may seem almost silly to find room for the real story. The Church may be whispering an invitation to personal preparation, but the world is downright screaming its invitations to sales, last-minute shopping, hysteria over the right present for the right person,

---

7   The reader goes by the name Theophilus, which literally translated means "one who loves God." Some scholars have suggested Luke was writing to a specific person, while others suggest he was offering a kind of general address to all those who are lovers of God. In either case, the exact recipient of the letter, whether individual or group, does not diminish the impact of Luke's intent.

beautiful Christmas cards laden with photos of the year gone by, packages, trees, bows, decorations, stress, exhaustion, and a sense of failure if it all does not come out exactly the way we had pictured it.

Compiling Luke and the other gospel accounts helps us with both of these challenges. We can let that orderly story help each of us put our lives in order. We can see his word as an invitation to put the brakes on those things that may not be as important as we once thought and instead hold fast to those things of infinite value. For Luke, and those of us preparing for Christmas, the thing of value is the real story with its real purpose: to draw us ever more deeply into a relationship with God in Christ.

Each day may seem a bit like the call for a garage sale. Our job, with God's help, is to take the time to look around and determine what is trash worth pitching away and what is treasure worth keeping, at any costs.

— *Preparing Room* —

Open your heart to pieces of the Advent and Christmas story that may be different than those you have always held in your mind's eye. Today, set aside time to begin sorting through the trash and treasures of these days. What could be tossed that would make a bit more room for God? What could be held just a bit more closely to open your heart even more?

A Prayer

God, in your almighty power you have so ordered that world that, left without the scourge of human sin and selfishness, all creation would glorify you.

Give me time and space this day to simply think on you and all of your gifts to your children.

Help me to discern those places of wasted energy and time, and have the courage to let them go, and give me the same gift to embrace more fully the precious jewels you have entrusted to my care.

That, having cast aside the trash and held fast to the treasure, I may indeed do as I am intended to do: glorify you.

Amen.

The Best-Laid Plans

In the sixth month the angel Gabriel was sent by God to a town in Galilee called Nazareth, to a virgin engaged to a man whose name was Joseph, of the house of David. The Virgin's name was Mary.

—Luke 1:26–27

In 1789, the poet Robert Burns wrote a poem entitled, "To a Mouse, on Turning Her Up in Her Nest with the Plough." He was evidently inspired to write this piece of verse after he accidentally turned over the nest of a mouse, while working on his own farm. It offers sympathy to a little mouse who has had her little home, and thus life, turned upside down when a human carelessly destroys her little nest. An oft-quoted line from the poem goes:

> But little Mouse, you are not alone,
> In proving foresight may be in vain:
> The best laid schemes of mice and men
> Go often askew,
> And leave us nothing but grief and pain,
> For promised joy![8]

Luke tells us something that was quite common in Mary's day. We learn of a young virgin who was pledged to be married to a man named Joseph. No one knows the exact ages of Mary and Joseph, but it was common for a young woman to find herself pledged in marriage in her early teens. It was also expected that the young

---

8   Robert Burns, "To a Mouse, on Turning Her Up in Her Nest with the Plough," (1789), stanza 7.

woman be a virgin. Then we see something very uncommon: God sends the angel Gabriel to upset the apple cart. We know what follows—the scheme laid down had, as Burns wrote, gone "askew." We have decorated that moment in our heads with songs, poems, art, and images that would lead us to believe how wonderful it was. But was it really?

The plans of Joseph and Mary's families were basically the same as every other well-meaning Jewish family in Nazareth: have children, let them grow, have them marry without scandal, have grandchildren, and continue the plan. For Mary, all of that was about to change. Placed before her was the challenge of becoming the most famous unwed mother of all time, and with it the scandal that would follow. The plan for a quiet life of wifedom and motherhood was simply not to be. There would certainly be moments of great joy, but we all know that parts of that plan would be torn asunder by the human savagery that awaited the child she would soon hold in her womb.

My hunch is that many of you reading now have, at one time or another, had your best-laid plans go askew. The college or graduate school you had *hoped* to attend does not accept you. The one you *did* attend proves to be too much a challenge and you are forced to drop out. The one with whom you had *hoped* to spend the rest of your life disappoints and the relationship dies. The job or business you had *hoped* would succeed does not. The experiment with drugs or alcohol turns to an addiction. The unexpected, unmarried pregnancy of your child. The child who runs away. The spouse who betrays. The accident or illness that appears. For most who live past one score and five, plans that go askew are as much a part of life as those that come to be, but what do we do then?

Unfortunately, unrealized plans, like dreams, can paralyze the human spirit. In 2004 a wonderful comedy film came out, *Napoleon Dynamite*. There are several interesting characters in the movie, all of whom offer a bit of a moral lesson for teens and adults alike. One in particular is Napoleon's uncle, Rico. While we do not get the entire story, we learn that during a high school football game he failed in a pass attempt to win the big game. Thus, his plans of playing college ball and being a hero in his hometown for the rest of his days were dashed. He spends all of his free time videotaping himself throwing passes, and then he runs the video back again and again, showing it to friends and relatives to prove that he really could have made it. At one point he confesses to his nephew Kip, "Ohhhh, man I wish I could go back in time. I'd take state." Of course, he does not.

Over the years of my pastoral ministry, I have met a number of Uncle Ricos: people whose plans were sidetracked and who simply cannot go on. But Mary found a way forward. The angel came and, as we will see in the next chapter, he brings a bit of news. Mary still is the most famous mother of all human history (for Christians and non-Christians alike).

Failing to let go of plans that do not go our way can dampen, hamper, or even destroy our ability to go on with life. If there is anything the experienced Christian knows about God, it is that He is not a God of dead-ends, but of beginnings. In the hands of God, a failed business does not mean the end of a vocation. A troubled marriage does not have to mean divorce. A broken marriage does not have to mean the end of love. A wayward child does not have to mean the end of that child's future. Cancer does not have to mean death. Even death, in the hands of God, does not have to mean the story is over. For God, the words "The End" never have to roll across the screen.

The key to living beyond the human tendency to run to "the end" is a kind of partnership with God. God is always willing to make the story better, if we are willing to offer our disappointments, our skewed plans, and our losses into God's hands.

There is an Old Testament proclamation that beautifully tells what God offers the one who finds plans sidelined. King Darius is the one whose plans are sidelined. When he witnessed what God had done for Daniel, who had spent the night in the lions' den, he declared of Daniel's God, "For He is the living God and He endures forever; His kingdom will not be destroyed, His dominion will never end. He rescues and He saves."[9]

For that good news we have nothing to offer but our gratitude for the hope yet to come.

— *Preparing Room* —

What about you? What plans did not go your way? Have you let that disappointment go? If not, why? Better yet, why not do it today? And then, see what God offers in return.

A Prayer

O Sovereign Lord,
When plans are ruined, help me;
When loved ones disappoint, hold me;
When joy is dashed, restore me;
When dreams become nightmares, strengthen me;
When all seems lost, remind me . . .
That in Your hands a mass of hopelessness,
Can become a work of art no eye can now see . . .
But remind me as well, that to see that work,
I must release what I hold as my pain,
Into Your promise of healing and hope.
Amen.

---

9 Daniel 6:26–27a. For the entire story, read Daniel chapter 6.

Meet and Greet

And he came to her and said, "Greetings, favored one! The Lord is with you."

—Luke 1:28

As a parish priest who has served various ministry settings in six different states over the years, I have been thrust into the presence of new faces and experiences more times than I can recount. When my wife, Laura, and I arrive in a new ministry setting, one of the ways we have tried to get to know those we are called to serve better is to host what we call a "Meet and Greet." Granted, it is a rather fabricated gathering in a limited amount of time, often with refreshments, with dozens of names and faces that are hard to hold onto only minutes after the experience is over. However, every single meeting that takes place, every single new experience, has the potential to change my life or that of my new acquaintance, if we choose to go beyond the meet and greet.

Mary, as far as we know, had never encountered an angel. Gabriel showing up meant the news was big, important. In all of scripture he only shows up in two other places: as the angel who interprets Daniel's dreams and as the one who predicts the birth of John the Baptist.[10] Mary had no way of knowing what was to follow, but clearly this was a new experience.

Despite my willingness to move about, I can be a bit of a fuddy duddy; I do not eagerly embrace new things. I have a favorite pair of shoes, shorts, pants, a favorite chair, film, book, and I

10 Daniel 8:16–26, 9:20–27; Luke 1:11–20.

can tend to get too much into a routine that I miss opportunities that come my way. I know many people who are part of the old fogey club I tend to run to at times. An unwillingness to meet and greet newness can also lead one into a host of ruts that creep into work, relationships, even leisure time. Over time, these ruts can become graves from which it is hard to escape.

While God certainly works in and through things that have been and are, it is also clear that a key *modus operandi* is to break through with new friends, relationships, and experiences. During his teaching years, Jesus spoke of His bringing a new covenant. He introduced His followers to a new command and He said those that followed Him would experience new birth.[11]

A few years back, on a Father's Day, I got the bug to go out with my youngest son on a kayak adventure. When I lived directly on the Gulf of Mexico I kayaked with each of my three children, but had yet to go on the bayou that was only a mile away from our newer home in Texas. This urge was on the heels of preaching three different morning services. I had been up since before dawn, I was a bit tired, but something urged me to pull out the boats, wash them off, and go on the roughly five-mile trail. Within no time, my son and I were meeting and greeting flora and fauna that I had never before seen. By journey's end—arms a bit tired, energy a bit spent—I was glad I had this new experience to remind me that God's hand was stretching into parts of a bayou that I could only reach by boat and paddle.

We know that despite the news that popped up on her doorstep, Mary did not turn away. Staying put allowed her to hear the other part of Gabriel's message: she was favored and God was with her.

That is often how God works when we open ourselves to new experiences. Fortunately, God does not limit his presence to Gothic cathedrals, meeting halls, or large tents. God may often whisper to us in music, poetry, film, relationships, nature, smells, or a good meal.

---

11 Matthew 26:28; Mark 14:24; Luke 22:20; John 13:34; John 3:3.

Is God calling you to a new experience, relationship, or way of life? Angels come in all kinds of ways, as does God's voice. Perhaps if you are not afraid to meet and greet something or someone new, you may also hear God's good news, "I am with you."

— *Preparing Room* —

Are you finding yourself in a rut? In your marriage or friendships? In your work? Your church? In the free time God has given you? Why not take the time to open yourself up to something new? Maybe in doing so you will come to know how very favored you are by God and how He is right there beside you.

A Prayer
O God, whose reason rules the world,
Who formed the starry heights above,
Timeless, time's chain far forth you hurled,
Unmoved, gave all things power to move.
Prevailed on by no outside cause
To fashion all reality;
Ideas of love and mental laws
moulded the noble world we see.
Your nature perfect beauty, thus
You made the world in tenderness
With sights and sounds to conjure us
To love the source of loveliness.
You named the primal elements
Of earth and water, air and fire,
And balanced out their influence
That none might lower be or higher.
O Father, give me power to climb
And wash in fountains filled with light,

Weighed down no more by things of time,
Lit by your shining in the night.
The sight of you begins our day,
With you its evening we shall spend;
You carry us, and lead the way,
The journey, and the journey's end.
Amen.

—Boethius, d. 524[12]

---

12 Michael Counsell, comp. *2000 Years of Prayer* (Harrisburg, PA: Morehouse, 1999), 35–6.

Troubles, Fears, and Wonders

But she was much perplexed by his words and pondered what sort of greeting this might be.

—Luke 1:29

We know that God chose Mary. She was special, particular. There was something God wanted to do with and in Mary. Some would say she was perfect, free of any human frailty that so plagues us. Yet we see Mary's brush with humanity in this very moment. At the good news greeting from Gabriel, she reacts as perhaps any of us would. We are told she was "troubled" and "wondered" what "kind of greeting this might be."

Now from the outside in, perhaps most of us would say, "Well, if an angel had just appeared, told me I was favored by God and that He was with me, I would not be troubled about anything!" Easily said, but that is not what happened. When the King of creation picks you out with a personal telegram, you know something is up. Maybe you are in trouble, maybe not. Either way, whatever certainty you had about how this was going to turn out might be tinged a bit with a sense of foreboding trouble—another word for that would be fear. Good old Gabriel clearly sensed that.

Take a breath. Of what are you afraid? When I was younger my fears were a bit different: the boogeyman and ghosts, getting crushed by the offensive line or bullied in junior high. As I have grown older, I would like to say I have shed all those fears, but they have merely morphed into different ones: the well-being of my children, wife, and parents; financial security; health; and world peace.

The reality is most of those things of which I am afraid are basically beyond my control. It is interesting that in many places throughout scripture, when God shows up the leading message is "Do not be afraid."[13]

How we actually get to that point, I will touch on in the next meditation. For now, let it rest within you that *even* Mary had her difficult moments. *Even* Mary was troubled when God poked into her world. Some see fear as sinful or wrong. The feeling of fear is not, in and of itself, sinful—unless it keeps one from doing what they should do, or more importantly what God would have them do. When fear melts into cowardice, we can be sure the self has stepped in front of God, and that is sin.

Mary had not experienced God in this way and she had every right to be troubled by the moment. Being troubled, being fearful in response to these words, is part of being human, but none of us wants to live in fear. Mary allowed her fear to turn into something called wonder. That feeling shifted because Mary chose to let what she was feeling come to the surface, and she dealt with what it was.

Only Mary could have told what happened that night, and somewhere in her telling she was bold enough to say, "When the angel showed up it was downright scary!" Good for her. For today, let the uneasiness, the fears come to the surface and face them. Maybe once you do, rather than see them as the victorious enemy, you can begin to see them as a challenge to overcome. You can begin to wonder how to go from here.

── *Preparing Room* ──

Today is a day to face. Name your fears. Make a list. Put them down and then ask God to help you let Him pluck them one by one and turn fear to wonder so that with His grace the fears will subside and peace will reign within you.

---

13 Genesis 26:24; Deuteronomy 1:21, 29; John 14:27.

A Prayer

Grant that we here before thee may be set free from the fear of vicissitude and the fear of death, may finish what remains before us of our course without dishonor to ourselves or hurt to others; and, when the day comes, may die in peace. Deliver us from fear and favour, from mean hopes and cheap pleasures. Have mercy on each in his deficiency; let him be not cast down. Support the stumbling on the way, and give at last rest to the weary. *Amen.*

—Robert Louis Stevenson, d. 1894[14]

---

14 Counsell, 417.

The Only Thing to Fear . . .

The angel said to her, "Do not be afraid, Mary, for you have found favor with God."

— Luke 1:30

President Franklin D. Roosevelt tried to calm a trembling nation by saying, "The only thing we have to fear is fear itself." He was not that far off. Though Mary was troubled as she chose not to run from something new, she also chose not to let fear consume her. Somehow, the tremble that was surely in her fingers and hands turned to wonder. There is an old Welsh prayer that says, "From ghoulies and ghosties and long-leggety beasties and things that go bump in the night, good Lord, deliver us!" That is a good prayer for kids, but it took more than a prayer to move Mary out of the fear she must have faced. The remedy for that fear must have already been simmering in her heart, giving her the gift of being ready for what the angel had to offer next.

We already know that she was favored. Gabriel began with that. He must have sensed her troubles and tells her the remedy to fear, "Do not be afraid," and, just to nail the point home, "Remember, you are favored." It was another way of saying, "Whatever troubles you have right now, you are not alone. God is right here in it with you, and He will see you to the other side."

I remember once as a child being terribly frightened by a loud noise in our basement. My only reaction was to yell, alerting my parents upstairs. I ran toward their open arms of protection. When it came time for my own children to undergo some of the minor surgeries of childhood, it was the comfort of a parent nearby that they wanted. When my son lost his memory for several hours after a concussion, I remember that, as we waited on doctors and nurses in the emergency room, he did not want to be left alone. Fortunately, he did remember his parents. When I am expecting what could be bad news by phone, I always want my wife nearby for comfort. I have prayed with many a church member as surgery approached, but when it was time for the priest to go, they always wanted a loved one there to hold their hand and be there when they woke. Companionship eases these kinds of fears, perhaps takes them away altogether.

That is what the angel is saying to Mary. Can you let that message address the fears that you listed at the end of the last chapter? There is a wonderful, beautiful passage in the First Epistle of John that reads, "Perfect love casts out all fear."[15] Remember the words of the Psalm, "Yea, though I walk through the valley of the shadow of death, I will fear no evil." Why? The next verse: ". . . for thou [God] art with me."[16]

Of course, that ability to embrace the companionship of the One whose other name is Love, does require a bit of faith. We will unpack that more in the pages ahead. For now, remember you are not alone. Asked to go to the boss's office? God is with you. Call from the police in the middle of the night? God is with you. The diagnosis letter from the doctor's office arrives? God is with you. God is with you before, during, and will be, to the other side of whatever valley you face. As God was with Mary, God is with you.

— *Preparing Room* —

Time to make some more room. Make a list of those things of which you are afraid. Take each fear one by one, take the hand of God, and face each and every one with His perfect love that drives away all fear.

---

15 1 John 4:18.
16 Psalm 23:4 (KJV).

A Prayer

I want Thee near dear Lord,
In confusion and perplexity, I want Thee near;
In loss and tribulation, I want Thee near;
In love tested and love lost, I want Thee near;
In betrayal and pain, I want Thee near;
In insurmountable challenges and unfathomable
   odds, I want Thee near;
In sickness and pain, I want Thee near;
In the terror of the night, I want Thee near;
In death and the end, I want Thee near;
Thus, by Thy mercy, give me all I need to know
That Thou always have been, always are, and
   always will be . . . near.
Amen.

And Now . . .

And now, you will conceive in your womb and
bear a son . . . .

—Luke 1:31a

I have been fortunate to be the beneficiary of resources that
allowed me to attend undergraduate, graduate, and post-graduate
work. Each program was filled with challenges of mind, body,
and spirit. At the end of each came the graduation—the moment
of being finished, but not complete. Graduation meant, "And
now, time to put that thing for which you have been preparing
to good use."

I have an old friend who has been a fishing captain for years.
He did not go out one day, buy a boat, and set up his charter business. It took years of training, preparation, trial and error before
he could wear that title, Captain. I have friends who are physicians,
attorneys, business people, bankers, teachers, and craftsmen: none
of them woke up one morning and began their craft, their vocation. It took training, taking on some of the things necessary to
learn the job, and getting things out of the way that might inhibit
their ability to go forward.

We see a shift in the early part of their story; the two words
"and now" mark a change. Once Mary was able to move past
resisting the new, facing her fears, and letting God deal with them,
the story moves from introduction to plan, from training for graduation to graduation, from graduation to what comes after graduation: "And now, you will conceive."

In these last few meditations we have been dealing with these
same things that Mary had to deal with: troubles, fears, and how

to get past them. It is one thing to say it, another to believe it, and quite another to act on it.

If you have been letting God wrestle with you during these last few meditations, I wonder if you are ready to take the next step. I wonder if you have really graduated? I wonder if you have really let the fears go? It goes without saying that God wants to live in us and work through us, but have we made room enough for him to do so? Are you ready for the "And now . . ."?

The Legend of Bagger Vance is a film about a fictional golf tournament set in 1930s Savannah, Georgia. The mythical match takes place between golf greats Bobby Jones, Walter Hagen, and a hometown boy named Rannulph Junuh. When he was a kid, he had great potential, but a tour of duty during World War I took the spunk out of him. His psychological wounds replace his love of golf with alcohol and gambling. Throughout this part of his life he keeps trying to find purpose, but he is fearful what that purpose may be. Then a shift occurs when his girlfriend invites him to the exhibition match with Jones and Hagen.

During the match, with only a few holes left, Junuh has taken the lead. As the game creeps toward the end, he trails behind. His tee shot on the seventeenth hole goes deep into the woods. When he enters the forest in search of his ball, he begins to panic. The mist creeping out of the ground reminds him of the battlefields where he had fought and watched others die. He begins to shake and he drops his club.

He spots his ball, but he is ready to quit, remembering why he turned from golf to the bottle in the first place. At that moment his golfing mentor finds him and asks which club he would like from his bag. He tells Junuh that his problem has to do with grip, not his golf grip, but the grip that the past holds on him.

"Ain't a soul on this entire earth ain't got a burden to carry he can't understand," Bagger consoles. "You ain't alone in that. But you've been carrying this one long enough. It's time to lay it down."

Junuh admits, "I don't know how!"

Bagger says, "You got a choice. You can stop, or you can start walking right back to where you've been and just stand there. It's time for you to come out of the shadows, Junuh! It's time for you to choose!"

"I can't," Junuh spits back.

"Yes you can," Bagger says. "You're not alone. I'm right here with you. I've been here all along. Now play the game. Your game. The only one you were meant to play. The one that was given to you when you came into this world. Now's the time!"[17]

Mary found her time. Is it yours? Have you really graduated? Are you ready to move past troubles and fears? Perhaps overcome a past that has held you back, held you down, one that has not necessarily gripped you, but one from which you have not yet released your grip?

Is it time to find a purpose that is not based on what you believe cannot be, but on what God wants to conceive in and through you? If so, then get ready, because what is next are two power-packed words: "And now!"

— *Preparing Room* —

Have you really released those fears and worries, those troubles? If so, then you have "graduated." What fills that space, that room after the two words, "And now"?

A Prayer

As the compass-needle's arms
point to North, South, East and West,
so the cross, through life's alarms
help us choose the way that's best.
Thank you, Lord, that you provide

---

17 Craig Brian Larson and Andrew Zahn, *Movie-Based Illustrations for Preaching and Teaching: 101 Clips to Show or Tell* (Grand Rapids, MI: Zondervan, 2003), 108–9.

This clear compass-cross to guide.
Where life's meaning is obscure,
through the valley of deep shade,
eyes are blind and hearts unsure;
Christ, our Sun, shine through to aid,
showing where before us lies
journey's end in paradise.
Transitory earthly things
break like bubbles in the breeze,
hopes dry up like desert springs,
plans may crash like rootless trees.
Drench dry land, O Lord, with rain,
till we hear the harvest grain.
Countless voices seek to guide,
many paths there are to choose,
if we turn to either side
firm ground soon our feet will lose.
Take us by the hand, we pray,
lead us on the narrow way.
Lord, through dusty ways ahead,
save the stumbling, here below,
be on every path we tread,
show lost sheep which way to go.
Guide us through the sheepfold's door,
till we come to joy once more.
Amen.

—Ernest Yang Yin-liu, b. 1934[18]

---

18 Counsell, 466.

Remember Jesus

. . . and you will name him Jesus.

—Luke 1:31b

About once a year, surveys come out in the United States about the most popular names chosen for babies. It is usually accompanied by names that are not so often chosen. If you are a student of culture, you will notice that those who are often in the public eye tend to choose names that will bring even more attention to them. Knowing the reality of how young people can be, particularly teens, I sometimes wonder what parents are thinking when they choose a name so odd or out of step with the norm; surely their child will be a target on the playground or in the locker room. At those times, I think sometimes it would help for someone to step in and tell them, "Here is the name of your new baby."

Mary, once she has passed her "and now" moment, is told the baby she will conceive will be named Jesus. No ifs, ands, or buts. Gabriel says it right out: "He will be named Jesus." If we bear the name Christian, we need to get this part of the story clear: Jesus Christ is the center and core of the Christian faith.

This Jesus was a historical figure, born in a particular time, in a particular place, of a particular race and gender. He came as he came and was as he was. If we are to follow him, we have freedom to raise our doubts and questions about who he was and what he came to do, but we do not have the freedom to change any of that to better suit our purposes and preferences.

I have had reason to smile when watching old films about the life and times of Jesus. Max von Sydow's version, *The Greatest Story Ever Told*, portrays a Jesus with white skin, blue eyes, and a lovely Shakespearean accent. In that particular film, the Jesus portrayed is often weak of manner and speech, appears to be wasting away almost from the start, and almost constantly has an otherworldly look. I have entered and preached at African American churches where I have seen a Jesus with black skin, an afro hairstyle, and clearly afro-centric features. There are similar paintings or images of an Asian Jesus. In recent years, some feminist theologians have emphasized Jesus's feminine qualities. Some theologians have tried to portray the single Jesus as gay.

These various portrayals of Jesus help us to understand why we try and mold Jesus into the person we might want him to be, but that is a slippery slope. Once you begin changing Jesus, it is easy to change, disregard, or weaken the things he said, things he taught, and things he demanded into things more suitable for our own ears. My mentor, John Claypool, used to tell me, "The problem with some theologians in our time is that they may teach that we were created in the image of God, but too often we try and return the favor!"

As I suggested in the preface, let us take Jesus for who he was, not for who we might like him to be. He was born in the ancient Middle East, therefore his skin would have been darker than anyone in the European, North American, or Asian territories, and lighter than anyone on the continent of Africa.[19] As a carpenter for all of his adult life, he would have had to be strong and sinewy, with rough, calloused hands. He was not androgynous, but he certainly possessed a mix of both masculine and feminine traits. As far as we know, he remained single all of his life. This was the Jesus of Christianity and the fulcrum for all that balances within the realm of our faith, which rests not primarily with the institutional church, human opinion, or speculation, but upon the person of Jesus.

I was smacked in the face with this just after my first year of seminary. I had been asked by one of my professors to pick up the

---

19 It is interesting to note that both Creationists and Evolutionists increasingly agree that the cradle of human existence was, however, northern Africa.

late Krister Stendahl, renowned New Testament scholar, at the airport. Retired as Bishop of Sweden, Dr. Stendahl was then serving as the chaplain at Harvard. For a budding seminarian, it was a wonderful opportunity to be with one of the great minds of the Church. However, once the moment came, I was caught off guard by what I can only describe as a mild-mannered presence.

I had just spent an entire year studying, debating, and reflecting on Church history, theology, and Church politics. I was used to getting tangled in lots of discussion that centered on lots of things that did not directly include Jesus. I confess I found it interesting that Dr. Stendahl asked no questions about my opinions on some of the current divisions in the Church or my position on them. He did not quiz me on biblical theology or ask if I was diligently studying my Hebrew and Greek. Instead, he simply asked questions about me: where I was from, if I was married and had children, and whether they liked seminary. Within moments, I was put at great ease. Given this once-in-a-lifetime opportunity, just before we ended our time together, I asked the good bishop, scholar, and chaplain, "What advice would you give someone like me just finishing up his first year of seminary?"

There was a long pause, and then simply, "Remember Jesus. Remember Jesus and his Cross." He took another breath and then said, "Too often today all of our discussion, all of our stories, all of our jokes are about the Church and not Jesus. Yes, remember Jesus."

That may very well have been one of the most important things I learned in my three years of seminary training. From that day forward, anytime I began to take notes on a lecture in seminary or post-graduate school; anytime I wrote a personal letter to a friend, priest, or bishop; anytime I wrote in my personal journal, I would write the date at the top and then those two words: "Remember Jesus."

It was a reminder that following him, serving him, and trying to learn from him meant following, serving, and learning from the Jesus that *was* and *is*, not the Jesus of my own making.

Gabriel told Mary, "You will name him Jesus." She may have had choices about the clothes he would wear, the food he would eat, bedtime, playtime, chores, and family rules, but as to his name—as to who he essentially was—she had no say. Neither do we. Remember Jesus.

— *Preparing Room* —

Do you have images of Jesus in your heart that you have sketched? Are they consistent with who Jesus really was and is? Ask God to help prepare a place in your heart for the Jesus that He sent to us as He was— no ifs, ands, or buts.

A Prayer

Dear Jesus,
If it is You I am to follow, let it be You;
If it is You I am to know, let it be You;
If it is You I am to serve, let it be You;
Keep me from the Jesus of my dreams,
  visions, creations;
And grant me a humble mind, body,
  and heart to
Follow, know, and serve
The Jesus You are so I may know
The child of God You call me to be.
Amen.

Good News

"He will be great, and will be called the Son of the Most High, and the Lord God will give to him the throne of his ancestor David. He will reign over the house of Jacob forever, and of his kingdom there will be no end."

—Luke 1:32–33

Today I ate lunch in an English pub that is older than the birth of the United States. Two nights ago, I watched a play in a theater that was built in 1705. I truly enjoy visiting historical places, whether Stonehenge or Mount Vernon, the Tower of London or Istanbul's Blue Mosque, the Cathedral of Notre Dame or Gettysburg. Walking through, breathing in historical places is almost a hallowed, spiritual experience—to step where those we view from modern eyes lived their lives and died their deaths.

What if we could look forward? What if we could stand in the home we just purchased and see in our mind all the things that would take place there? What if we knew all that followed our first day on the job? What if someone told us who we, or our children, would befriend or marry and what they would be? What if what would someday be history could be given to us before it happened?

For instance, we might take some relief in knowing our children would outlive us and have healthy, prosperous lives. We might get excited knowing that beginning in the mailroom might lead to the board room. We might take delight in knowing the first date will end in marriage at the altar! Of course, we might not like what we learn as well.

In Mary's case, Gabriel does not hit her with all the news at once. For this announcement moment, he will only give her the

Good News. He tells her this child will be special. He is going to rise in power, and this power will not last for a season, but for all time. Surely this news would bring joy to any mother's heart.

As a young Jewish girl, Mary would know about the scriptural promises and prophecies that God would one day send a Messiah to take up the throne of David. In other words, Mary was being introduced to the fact that she was to be part of the vessel that carried these prophecies to fruition.[20]

I know many clergy and scholars in our day that seem to almost take delight in casting doubt on crucial pieces of the Christian story. Was Mary a virgin upon the birth of Jesus? Were Jesus's miracles real or just mirages? Did Jesus really rise from the grave? That is the easier path though, is it not? Is it not easier to discount things that may be difficult to believe rather than to believe them?

Any twenty-first-century Christian will rightly, academically, and thoughtfully work through their faith. Yet at some point, the leap to belief must take place or one just remains floundering somewhere between truth and confusion. At this point, we do not see the young Mary tossing up a hand and saying, "Now hold on, wait just a minute. I just cannot believe all of this." Nope. She lives into the faith entrusted to her nation, her people, her family—entrusted to her.

I once read a story that during the Cold War, when Communism still had its grip on Eastern Europe, Queen Elizabeth of Belgium made a state visit to Warsaw. She was assigned a Polish protocol officer to accompany her to Roman Mass.

As they traveled to church, she asked him, "Are you a Catholic?"

At which point he answered, "Believing, but not practicing."

"I see," she replied. "Then you must be a Communist."

He said, "Practicing, your majesty, but not believing."[21]

I wonder if the officer's response strikes a chord. Do not many people in our day practice, but not believe; or perhaps believe, but do not practice their faith? An old friend of mine used to say that when it came to Christians, he knew those who would wear the

---

20 Some of these prophecies include 2 Samuel 7:16; Psalm 89:3, 4; Isaiah 9:7; Jeremiah 33:17; Daniel 2:44; Micah 4:7.

21 Edward Hays, *A Pilgrim's Almanac* (Easton, KS: Forest of Peace Books, 1989), 174.

badge but not live the life, and those who would live the life but not wear the badge. Would it not be a better thing to believe and practice; to wear the badge and live the life? To continue to flip flop between belief and practice at our own whim can lead one's faith to be overwhelmingly self-centered.

Those in my business often joke about the "C and E Christians"— Christmas and Easter. Of course, I am happy to have people attend worship whenever their spirit (or family member) urges them to do so, but is that gap between the truths of our faith and weakness of the human spirit to embrace them helped in any way by keeping belief and practice from one another?

What Mary received from Gabriel was really good news. It was good news to her because she was already one who both believed and practiced the faith entrusted to her.

We can do the same, you know. Once we have jumped the hurdles of doubt and the distractions of details about specifics, then the only thing left is a leap of faith. When we make it, as did Mary, we can smile as she did, at the good news.

— *Preparing Room* —

Practicing but not believing? Believing but not practicing? Does either of these speak to you? Why not open your heart to a Spirit that will melt the two together and allow for you the gift of Good News.

A Prayer

I beg you, most loving Saviour, to reveal yourself to us,
that knowing you we may desire you, that desiring you
we may love you, that loving you we may ever hold you
in our thoughts.
Amen.

—Columbanus, d. 615[22]

---

22 Robert Van de Weyer, *Celtic Fire* (London: Darton, Longman & Todd, 1990).

Bad News

Mary said to the angel, "How can this be, since I am a virgin?"

—Luke 1:34

Mary's question above is not a moment of doubt, it is an honest one. She is a virgin. How can she be with child if she has not had physical intimacy with a man? It was almost a moment of innocent curiosity.

Having just heard the good news, Mary is sensing what could be very, very bad news indeed. The 2009 movie *The Nativity Story* portrayed this part of the story rather well. Despite all the good news, the reality is that Mary is found with child without the benefit of marriage. What followed in the film was the gossiping and whispering. This most famous of teen pregnancies meant scandal not only for Mary and her family, but also Joseph and his family.

There are lots of things one can take from this small but important piece of the story. At least one lesson is a cautionary note against what Jesus admonished as sinful: casting judgment on others.

In his sermon on the mount, Jesus warned, "Do not judge, so that you may not be judged. For with the judgment you make you will be judged, and the measure you give will be the measure you get" (Matthew 7:1–2). Now in all fairness, Jesus was not suggesting one cannot make judgments about what is generally right and wrong. Jesus was not saying that if you witnessed child abuse you should reserve judgment. He was not saying to turn a blind eye to infidelity or injustice. It was his way of telling all of us, as one might before a fencing match, *"En garde!"* Guard your heart about making hasty judgments when you do not know the full story. If everyone in Mary's day knew the whole story, what was really going on in her womb, would they not call off their judgment? If we do not know all the details of the story, should we not put our hearts on guard as well?

I have counseled many a couple in times of troubled marriage. Many times, the public reaction is to blame one partner over another when, behind closed doors, there is a fuller story. I know loving parents who experience shame over the waywardness of a child and the pain that others inflict by evaluating their parenting, when there was no wayward parenting motive or practice. I have good friends who spent time behind bars and found, upon their release, that it was virtually impossible for others to let go of their judgment long enough to establish a friendship, offer a job, or even share a conversation. I know many people who have lived through the "scandal" of an out-of-wedlock child. Perhaps, while others look askance, God takes delight in the beating heart of another child to love.

"How can this be?" Mary asked. The reality is she may not have fully liked the answer she received or its implications, but she moved all of that aside. The rest is up for us to judge—or not.

— *Preparing Room* —

Have you judged another? Are you doing so now? Do you know the full story? Even if you do, is that other worthy of any measure of judgment you might use? Remember what Jesus said, as you measure it out, it will be measured to you. Why not let that measure out of your heart, so that there is more room to love, and love without judgment?

A Prayer

O God of love, we pray Thee to give us love: love in our thinking, love in our speaking, love in our doing, and love in the hidden places of our souls; love of our neighbors, near and far; love of our friends, old and new; love of those whom we find it hard to bear, and love of those who find it hard to bear with us; love of those with whom we work, and love of those with whom we take our ease; love in joy, love in sorrow; love in life and love in death; that so at length we may be worthy to dwell with thee, who are eternal love, Father, Son and Holy Spirit, for ever and ever. *Amen.*

—William Temple, d. 1944[23]

---

23 Counsell, 441.

Power Play

Now the birth of Jesus the Messiah took place in this way. When his mother Mary had been engaged to Joseph, but before they lived together, she was found to be with child from the Holy Spirit.

—Matthew 1:18

The angel said to her, "The Holy Spirit will come upon you, and the power of the Most High will overshadow you; therefore the child to be born will be holy; he will be called Son of God."

—Luke 1:35

Matthew and Luke have two takes on this piece of the story. As we have already noted, Luke, the historian, goes a bit more into detail than his fellow gospel writer, Matthew. They agree on the point that Mary's conception was the result of the work of the Holy Spirit. The "power," as Gabriel puts it, would move upon Mary's womb and plant new life within it—what theologians call the immaculate conception.

The Holy Spirit, I find in my work, is often hard for some people to grasp. Church members often have a greater grasp of a heavenly God, a parent who cares for his children, and a Jesus who, as we are seeing here, was born, walked the same earth that we do, and left behind teachings and work that still shape the face of that same earth. The Spirit remains a bit of mystery, but why?

In Holy Scripture, we are introduced to God's Spirit before we are introduced to the Second Person of the Trinity. Genesis 1:2 reports that "the earth was a formless void and darkness covered the face of the deep, while a wind from God swept over the face of the waters." This "wind" is God's Spirit, and like God and God's Son, a part of the Trinity. To try and unpack the Trinity in this little meditation is more than I want to do. Augustine once said, "The one who receives the Trinity will save his soul; but the One who tries to understand the Trinity will lose his mind!"[24] Let me save that for another day.

For now, what God wanted Mary to know was that she need not try to figure out how it would all happen. God's power, God's Spirit was going to work it all out.

How often is it that we humans doubt when God invites us into something with him, that God will not abandon us or leave us to our own resources? One could almost argue that the whole of the Judeo-Christian story is really an invitation to receive the constant companionship of God, an invitation to join God in his work and a promise to be with us. Jesus's last words to His disciples were, "And remember, I am with you always, to the end of the age" (Matthew 28:20). He lived out that assurance by sending the promised Holy Spirit.[25]

Perhaps it would be helpful to look at it this way. The Greek word Jesus used for the Holy Spirit was paraclete. It was a word that would have been known to Jesus's audience. Paraclete, sharing the same root as the word "parallel," was a term used by ancient Greek soldiers. In battle, the soldiers would go in twos, parallel to one another. When the enemy came, they could stand back to back, holding up shield and sword to cover their blind spots. Soldiers still had to do their own work, but they were not sent into battle alone.

In our day, we sometimes consider the words "power play" to have a negative connotation, as if someone got away with something because of the power they possessed. In this case, God did, but it was not an abuse of power. Ultimately, Mary had to agree to all that was being proposed, but she could not do it alone: she

24 This quote was taken from personal notes kept throughout the author's ministry.
25 John 16:5–16; Acts 2:1–13.

needed God. We forget sometimes that God is there to help us. So often we, like Mary, will require something outside of ourselves to make what seems impossible, possible.

That great evangelist of the last century, Corrie Ten Boom, once said, "I have a glove here in my hand. The glove cannot do anything by itself, but when my hand is in it, it can do many things. True, it is not the glove, but my hand in the glove that acts. We are gloves. It is the Holy Spirit in us who is the hand, who does the job. We have to make room for the hand so that every finger is filled."[26]

When you know God is calling on you to do something with God or to do something in or through you, do you think you are alone? Remember God's Spirit, God's Power, God's presence. Then, think again.

— *Preparing Room* —

Where in your life today are you asking Mary's question, "How will this be?" Can you make room for God's power play? God's Spirit? If not, why? If so, then do it and do it now.

A Prayer

Come Holy Spirit, Come.
How can I go on, but without You?
How can I bridge this gap, but without You?
How can I heal this pain, but without You?
How can I do this work, but without You?
How can I heal my friendship, but without You?
How can I restore my marriage, but without You?
How can I live with my loss, but without You?
How can I finish the race put before me, but without You?
Come Holy Spirit, Come.
Amen.

---

26 Corrie Ten Boom, *Each New Day* (Grand Rapids, MI: Revell, 2003), 96.

Facing the Scars

Her husband Joseph, being a righteous man and unwilling to expose her to public disgrace, planned to dismiss her quietly.

—Matthew 1:19

A few blocks from a London hotel where I once stayed, there are powerful words engraved into the stone on Exhibition Row next to the famous Victoria and Albert Museum. The plaque reads:

> The Damage to These Walls Is The
> Result Of Enemy Bombing During The
> Blitz Of The Second World War 1939–1945
> And Is Left As A Memorial To The Enduring
> Values Of This Great Museum In A Time of Conflict

Up and down the building's side are dozens of pockmarks made by shell pieces and shrapnel from the Third Reich's Air Force incessant bombing of London. As I looked at and touched the wounds in the stone, it was a humbling and emotional experience.

I live in a part of the United States where it is not uncommon for people to buy homes many would consider "fixer uppers." Instead of fixing these homes, the new owners choose to tear them down and replace them with new ones. They leave behind virtually no evidence of what might have been only bruised and broken.

As I alluded earlier, I think one of the many things that confirm the truths of Holy Scripture is that it tends to leave the pockmarks in the story. The story about Joseph in all of this is such a profound mark. The shame he must have felt in finding his betrothed with child must have been overwhelming. Furthermore, without benefit of any dreams or angelic visitations, can you imagine what he felt when Mary shared the news? And even if he did take hold of it all, can you imagine the sense of foreboding he must have felt knowing that the first born in their shared household was not his, but God's?

What was Joseph's plan? Quickly cover the pockmarks. Matthew is a bit tender here in suggesting that Joseph's motives were admirable. He did not want to subject Mary to public disgrace. Either way it would have been seen as disgraceful. If Joseph's plan had been put into action, Mary would potentially have been even more disgraced by being pregnant without benefit of husband or present father. So, noble or not, Joseph planned to put the pregnant Mary away and arrange a secret termination of the relationship. I think any of us would understand. Even if we would not go to his extremes, we might do our best to hide the details of the story to make them more palatable to the neighbors. But again, an angel popped up and straightened Joseph out: you are not going to change the story; you need to come to terms with the way things are, not the way you would like them to be.

As I have already noted, we have tidied up this story. I know the crèche we set up in our home each Advent has a figure of Joseph lovingly looking down on the child Jesus. The little figure does not have an asterisk that notes, "Originally, Joseph had intended to send Mary and her unborn child away so he did not have to deal with them."

Having worked intimately with people behind closed doors for nearly three decades, I do not know anyone who does not have some skeleton in their closet. I do not know anyone who is perfect.

I do not know anyone who does not have something they wish to God they had not done, or anyone who has not failed to do something that they wish to God they could go back and do over. We all have sins of commission and omission. We have in the words of the Apostle Paul, "all sinned and fallen short of the glory of God."[27] That includes dear father Joseph; that includes you and me.

When I was a kid, riding small motorized go-karts or motorbikes was something readily welcomed. One afternoon, I went out with a friend and we worked to juice up his little go-kart. Having done so, we both hopped on. He was driving and I was in the passenger seat—with no seatbelts. When he took a sharp turn, I did not. I fell out, rolled, and bounced over a patch of asphalt. When I stopped, stood up, and brushed myself off, it looked like I had been rolling in a patch of strawberries. I will leave the rest to your imagination.

Next stop—home. My mother and aunt were on the back porch. I did my best to hide my wounds, go inside, and patch them up. But by evening, it was clear no one would miss all my little scraped bits and pieces.

To this day, I have a little round circular scar on the upper side of my right hand. The skin is a bit darker there, a bit tougher. Every time I look at it, I remember the day I decided to make not one, but several wrong decisions. It also reminds me that we can learn from old wounds. Old wounds do and can heal when we expose them to healing light and air.

I once heard the writer Frederick Buechner say, "We are as sick as our secrets." What he meant, of course, is that we need to let light shine on the dark places of our lives. How many people suffer with quiet addictions? How many fail to share abuse they had waged upon them as a child? How many are ashamed of something a parent or a child did? Why do we hide these things? Shame? Embarrassment? Fear of what others may think? Here's a little theological response: so what?

---

27 Romans 3:23.

It is God, not others, to whom we answer for how we live our lives. It is God, not others, who has the power to deal with the dark places of our past or present. We may, like Joseph, prefer to put them away, but are we then dealing with them?

Those pockmarks on the wall of the Victoria and Albert Museum remind everyone who passes by that, in the words of my mentor John Claypool, "The worst things are not the last things." Sure, someone could have patched them up and filled them in, but when I pass by them, I am inspired.

What about you? Are there skeletons in your closet? Of course, there are. Do you have some old scars still waiting to be healed? Have you dealt with them? More importantly, have you allowed God to deal with them? Do not be tempted as Joseph was to put them away. Face them and, in doing so, find the strength that comes with being inspired by hope.

— *Preparing Room* —

Open the closet door; what skeleton do you find in there? What have you been tempted to put away? Are you ready to deal with it? Are you willing to let God help you face it? And heal it?

A Prayer

We thank you, Lord and Master, for teaching us how
to pray simply and sincerely to You and for hearing us
when we so call upon You. We thank You for saving
us from our sins and sorrows, and for directing all our
ways this day. Lead us ever onwards to yourself; for the
sake of Jesus Christ our Lord and Saviour. *Amen.*

—John of Kronstadt, d. 1908[28]

---

28 Counsell, 55.

U-Turn

But just when he had resolved to do this, an angel
of the Lord appeared to him in a dream and said,
"Joseph, son of David, do not be afraid to take Mary
as your wife, for the child conceived in her is from the
Holy Spirit."

—Matthew 1:20

When Joseph awoke from sleep, he did as the angel
of the Lord commanded him; he took her as his wife.

—Matthew 1:24

Joseph changed his mind. We do not know if he changed his
heart, but he did change his mind. The vision put before him was
like holding up a mirror and saying, "Do you really want to put
her away? Do you really want to get in the way of what God wants
to do in your family? Do you really want to put a speed bump
in the path of God's salvation for the world?" Joseph changed his
mind, and with that, he became a full-throated participant, which
of course leads one to believe that he did, in fact, change his heart
as well.

Not too long ago, I took a left turn and quickly found myself
going the wrong way on a one-way street. My oncoming friends
were quick to let me know with their horns and voices that I
needed to make a U-turn. The only way to safety was to follow
their advice. I had to change my direction.

When I was a university chaplain, I had a young student who
seemed, on the outside, to have everything going his way—a

bright personality, intelligent, attractive. One day he scheduled an appointment. The door closed, pleasantries were exchanged, and, within minutes, out came the tears. His combination of good looks and charm had allowed him to explore a world of sexual promiscuity. Even though an undergraduate, he began to unfold years of relationships that included infidelity, unwanted pregnancy, and the danger of sexually transmitted diseases. He felt trapped. He felt imprisoned by his lifestyle. It was as if, though clearly by his own choices, he felt there was no way forward.

When Joseph got a clear picture of what seemed to be a dead end, it was actually a stepping-stone to a new chapter in his life. He changed his mind; he changed his direction. He did a U-turn.

I wonder if you have ever felt this way? I wonder if you feel this way now? I wonder if because of things you have done or are doing that you think there is no hope, no possibility for redemption?

The 1954 movie *On the Waterfront* includes a powerful scene. Marlon Brando portrays former boxer, Terry Malloy, turned errand boy for the mob. His reflections on the mess in which he finds himself come to a head during a taxi ride with his former manager in the back of a cab. Legend says that the scene was not scripted; Brando chose to pour out his heart and feelings ad lib. He says, "I coulda had class! I coulda been a contender! I coulda been somebody! Instead of a bum, which is what I am."

The young man in my office felt like there were no other options but to continue down the increasingly damaging and painful road he was walking. But on that day, I held up a mirror. I agreed with him that this was no way to live one's life and that if he continued, there would be more heartache, guilt, and misery. Together, over a period of time, we worked through that valley and made it to the other side. He found not only forgiveness, but a new life.

Of course, it is one thing to see one's error or sin, but quite another to change direction and make that U-turn. Joseph awoke from his dream in full U-turn mode. We are told by Matthew that he did as the angel commanded him; he took Mary as his wife.

None of us caught in a trap of our own doing want to remain there. None of us want to wake up one morning and cry out, "But

I coulda been . . . ." The good news of our Christian hope is that with God's hand in our midst, we always have an opportunity for a new, fresh start.

Scripture is filled with promises for those who choose to make that U-turn. We do not have to live with the burden of the past. The Psalmist writes, "as far as the east is from the west, so far he removes our transgressions from us" (Psalm 103:12). John reminds his readers, "If we confess our sins, he who is faithful and just will forgive us our sins and cleanse us from all unrighteousness" (1 John 1:9).

So, there is a lot going on in this little scene. Joseph has one thing in mind. He is wrong about that thing. An angel holds up a spyglass to give him a vision of what could be, which quickly turns into a mirror that shows Joseph his chosen path was wrong. He realizes it, and turns in the opposite direction. And Joseph is now remembered not so much for his reluctance to run along with God, but his willingness to be guided by God onto a path in the right direction—what the Bible calls righteousness.

What might you see if Gabriel were to hold up a spyglass for you to see what could be in your life that is not yet, and then if he were to hold up a mirror so that you could see a wrong direction in which you might have turned?

— *Preparing Room* —

Is there a need for a U-turn in your life? What kind of turn might open a path of righteousness in your own life?

A Prayer

Have mercy on me, O God,
according to your steadfast love;
according to your abundant mercy
blot out my transgressions.
Wash me thoroughly from my iniquity,
and cleanse me from my sin.
For I know my transgressions,
and my sin is ever before me.
Against you, you alone, have I sinned,
and done what is evil in your sight,
so that you are justified in your sentence
and blameless when you pass judgment . . .
Wash me, and I shall be whiter than snow.
Let me hear joy and gladness;
let the bones that you have crushed rejoice.
Hide your face from my sins,
and blot out all my iniquities.
Create in me a clean heart, O God,
And put a new and right spirit within me . . .
Restore to me the joy of your salvation,
and sustain in me a willing spirit.
Amen.

—Portions of Psalm 51, David's Prayer
of Confession after being confronted
by the prophet Nathan with his sin
of adultery with Bathsheba

What's in a Name?

"She will bear a son, and you are to name him Jesus,
for he will save his people from their sins."

—Matthew 1:21

Now that Joseph is realigning his heart with God's purposes, the angel Gabriel goes on to unfold more of the story. He not only tells Joseph what he has already told Mary about naming the child, but goes on to unpack the consummate purpose behind this conception and soon-to-be birth.

The name Jesus is a Greek translation of the name Joshua that, literally translated, means "the Lord saves." Jesus had a primary mission—to save God's children, but from what? Our Judeo-Christian scriptures teach us that God did not intend Creation to be infiltrated by the power of sin and rebellion. God wanted and intended for Creation to be a celebration of unfiltered, unencumbered fellowship between God and his children, and the children with each other. But somewhere in the story the plans went awry and humans abused God's gift of freedom to choose. We decided to choose self over others.

If you know your Bible, you know that the first creatures were not tempted by an apple, but instead by a temptation ruled by self. "Eat and you will be like God," was the temptation.[29] I would suggest you not get caught up in the literal nature of the Genesis story. Let it speak for itself. The point of the story was that turning from God was the beginning of sin. And with that sin, Creation began to break down. Humans began to take almost an addictive

---

29 Genesis 3:5.

obsession with following self over others, over God. With that obsession, all the darkness that has been wrought on human history began.

Jesus came to save humankind from this power of sin. He came to give them the full mercy that comes with forgiveness that can only be offered by him; the freedom to live an abundant life that can only be given by him; and the grace that so fills this mercy and life that the fruit is eternal life, that can only be rewarded by him.

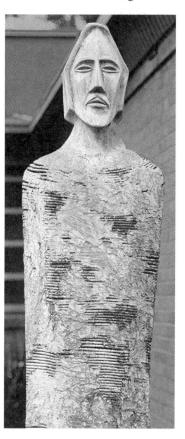

Jesus saves and came to save. Jesus surely came to do and offer many other things—ethical and moral teachings, calls to care and concern for others, appeals to cultural and social justice—but his primary mission was a spiritual one. All else that he did was offered to drive people toward his salvation. He did not come to make a better world; he came to make a new world. He did not come to make you and me better; he came to make us new.

Anglican scholar, John Stott, puts it well,

> "Salvation" is a wonderfully comprehensive term. It is a great mistake to suppose that it is merely a synonym for forgiveness. God is as much concerned with our present and future as with our past. His plan is first to reconcile us to Himself, and then progressively to liberate us

from our self-centeredness and bring us into harmony with our fellow men.[30]

As we must put aside our own notions of who Jesus was or is, we should also put away notions about what he came to do if they are inconsistent with his primary purposes for coming to be among us. Jesus came, as Gabriel puts it, to establish a kingdom that will last forever. A kingdom that falls not to the power of sin and death, but rises on their ashes built upon a foundation of grace, mercy, forgiveness, life, and eternal salvation.

As the old saying goes, "What's in a name?" What's in Jesus's name? The Lord saves. Jesus saves. And if you are willing, he will save you from the power of sin and from death itself.

— *Preparing Room* —

How have you viewed the primary mission of Jesus? Is He more than teacher? Prophet? Religious figure? Or is He, as Gabriel told Mary, a King? Your king? Is He, as Gabriel told Joseph, Savior—your Savior? Take some time to shed from your heart anything about Jesus that would take away from this power to save you or the ability to allow Him to be your King.

A Prayer

Jesus, remember me when you come into
your kingdom.
Amen.[31]

---

30 John Stott, *Basic Christianity* (Downer's Grove, IL: Inter-Varsity Press, 1971), 98.

31 These are the words of a thief on his own cross, uttered to Jesus in recognition of Jesus's mission (Luke 23:42). It is used as a prayer, and sometimes a song, in various religious traditions, often repeated several times to focus the mind, heart, and soul in the direction of surrender to Jesus, both as King and Savior.

Fill Her Up!

All this took place to fulfill what had been spoken by the Lord through the prophet: "Look, the virgin shall conceive and bear a son, and they shall name him Emmanuel," which means, "God is with us."

—Matthew 1:22–23

Matthew adds a bit of commentary to the story here.[32] He tells us that what is unfolding before Mary and Joseph is a fulfillment of a prophecy spoken by the prophet Isaiah sometime during the eighth century BCE. Much of the Hebrew Bible, though scripted to describe its own day, is forward looking. Much of it records the prophets, major and minor, who spoke words of what would someday come. Some of their prophecies were to be revealed in their own day, some within decades of their ministry, and others had a horizon yet unseen. Such was the case with the many prophecies about a Messiah who would come to save humanity from their sins and restore them to an unfettered relationship with God. Isaiah's words are such a prophecy.

There is in our own day no lack of fascination with predicting the future—whether it is a heads up on your day offered by your daily horoscope in the local paper or grand visions put forth by late-night televangelists. No question, many of us would like a peek into our future. However, most biblical prophecies had a much larger purpose than how one's day might unfold or even the precise moment when earth as we know it would come to a close.

---

32 Isaiah 7:14.

Prophecies were, for the most part, about unveiling God's purposes. That is what Matthew tells the reader of his gospel.

The opening salvo of the Jesus story does not begin with Mary, Joseph, and Gabriel; it goes back much further. It is the fulfillment of God's promise to come in the flesh and really show that God wants to walk among his children and be "with them," as Isaiah professes and Matthew reminds. What is happening through Mary and Joseph is not so much about the moment, but rather the fulfillment of a promise. Fulfillment and "filled up" really have the same meaning. Gabriel came to announce that Mary and Joseph were key players in "filling up" the promise of God.

Most readers probably remember a full-service gas station. I remember, more times than I can count, riding in the back seat of my parents' car, having them pull into a station, rolling down their window (there was a day when we rolled them down), and telling the attendant to "Fill 'er up." That meant the gas had run low and we needed to be refilled to continue our journey.

The moment where Gabriel, Joseph, and Mary intersect is not the end nor is it the beginning of the journey of our faith. It is a point, a blip on the heart monitor that reminds us that all throughout history, God is. It is important to stop and let prophecies like Isaiah's "fill us" with a kind of knowledge that the days we live fall on a much larger spectrum than how we use our own years. It is okay to stop before these kinds of stories and seek to be reminded that God is with us. God was with us way before we were, God is with us now, and God will be with us long into the future.

This is hopefully fuel for a human engine that may be tired, lonely, afraid; one that feels forgotten, abandoned, confused, or is terrified by present circumstances. Perhaps it is time to roll into the station of the story, hear Isaiah's words again, "God with us," and respond with our own "Fill 'er up," and allow that fuel to buoy you past the present and into the future. That is a prophecy I can live with; how about you?

— *Preparing Room* —

How is your heart opened by the knowledge that God's plan has been, and continues to be, "with us"? Are you tired? Lonely? Afraid? Do you feel alone? God promises to be with you. Can you open your heart to that promise?

A Prayer

You promise, O God to be with us;
When all is well, with us;
When all is unraveling, with us;
When celebrating, with us;
When mourning, with us;
When quivering in fear, with us;
When trembling in ecstasy, with us;
In horror and fear;
In joy and laughter;
In pain and pleasure;
In living and dying;
You promise, O God, to be with us;
Reveal my deep want to me,
That I may have a heart to let your promise fill me;
So the hope of your everlasting presence
Would grant me your everlasting peace.
Amen.

An Act of Balance

... but had no marital relations with her until she had borne a son; and he named him Jesus.

—Matthew 1:25

I suppose there are two equally skewed ways of looking at God's gift of sexual intimacy and, quite frankly, all physical intimacy that goes on between human beings. One way is to believe it is the ultimate human experience—the be all and end all, as the saying goes. Modern culture has done a fairly good job of that. Don't agree? Pick up a copy of *People* magazine, *Cosmopolitan*, or simply watch two hours of primetime television.

Another way is to shun this gift of God as unnatural: a necessary exercise limited for the purpose of procreation; something that should be shoved into closets, or deep in the bookshelves of the library; a topic deemed unsuitable for conversation. The traditional Church has done a fairly good job of this one. A good example would be the mythical suggestion that Mary remained a virgin all of her life—that she never experienced sexual intercourse, physical intimacy, and never bore more children, as if those things would in some way take away from her purity. But we know from Holy Scripture that she did, in fact, bear other children who were Jesus's siblings.

I should readily confess that I have been guilty of giving in to both extremes when it comes to my own understanding of this complex, terrifying, wonderful, frustrating, gentle, and joyful gift of God. But if neither extreme is a proper way to understand this gift, what is the proper way? Perhaps the little passage gives us a peek into one possible answer. We are told that Joseph did not have marital relations with Mary until she had given birth to Jesus. In other words, Joseph, whether inspired or instructed to do so, chose to abstain for a season in recognition of the holy work going on in the midst of his home, and, even more, in his dear wife's womb.

C. S. Lewis suggests that if anyone believes sexual morality, or immorality for that matter, is the core of Christian moral teaching, they are off center. Perhaps one way of digging even deeper into this passage is to understand how God's many gifts are manifested in physical pleasures that are to be enjoyed and savored, not gluttonized.

Throughout the Judeo-Christian story, fasting—a period of abstaining from food—has been associated with walking deeper into a holy life. During the Advent and Lenten seasons, it is common for Christians to purposely choose to abstain from some form of physical indulgence—perhaps even as simple as chocolate or wine; other times, fasting from food or drink on a day during the week. In any case, the purpose is to give greater attention to one's call to holiness. But the period of fasting comes to an end, and when it does there is celebration and a greater appreciation for the objects from which one abstained.

Understanding and perhaps enjoying physical gifts of pleasure from God is not so much about how much or how little, but more about achieving balance. Food, drink, intimacy, or physical training are all gifts from God. But the one who only eats, becomes a glutton; the one who only drinks, becomes a drunkard. Today, it is not uncommon to walk down the beach and see both extremes: women and men spilling out of tight-fitting swimwear and others who spend hours a day tending to abdominals and biceps, likely to the exclusion of time with family or friends. When excessive attention or time is given to one of these physical aspects of our life, then the opportunity for appreciating the gift's intrinsic holiness is completely lost.

The blessing before a meal is that moment where God is recognized for what is about to be enjoyed. The marriage service is offered to the couple who will not just enjoy a lifetime of physical intimacy, but emotional and spiritual intimacy as well.

Perhaps Joseph remembered the author's words in Ecclesiastes, "For everything there is a season, and a time for every matter under heaven . . . a time to embrace, and a time to refrain from embracing" (Ecclesiastes 3:1, 5). His decision did not mean "No, never," but, "Not now; later." God's gifts are not so much about the gift itself, but about God's love, God's word, and God's desire to draw us ever closer to him.

Let me turn back to C. S. Lewis once again. In his autobiography *Surprised by Joy: The Shape of My Early Life*, he wrote, "Joy is not a substitute for sex; sex is very often a substitute for Joy. I sometimes wonder whether all pleasures are not substitutes for Joy."[33] He was not, of course, suggesting that pleasures are a bad thing, but instead they are not, as I wrote at the beginning of this meditation, the be all and end all. They should instead be accepted, enjoyed, and appreciated, but should also be seen as only a hint of the pleasures and joy God will fully bestow. Perhaps that is why Lewis preached these words in a sermon entitled, "The Weight of Glory:"

> If there lurks in most modern minds the notion that to desire our own good and earnestly to hope for the enjoyment of it is a bad thing, I submit that this notion is no part of the Christian faith. Indeed, if we consider the unblushing promises of reward and the staggering nature of the rewards promised in the gospels, it would seem that Our Lord finds our desires not too strong, but too weak. We are half-hearted creatures, fooling about with drink and sex and ambition when infinite joy is offered us, like an ignorant child who wants to go on making mud pies in a slum because he cannot imagine what is meant by the offer of a holiday at the sea. We are far too easily pleased.[34]

---

33 C. S. Lewis, *Surprised by Joy: The Shape of My Early Life* (New York: Harcourt Brace Jovanovich, 1955), 170.

34 C. S. Lewis, "The Weight of Glory," in *The Weight of Glory and Other Addresses* (New York: HarperCollins, 2001), 26.

Too much or too little of a good thing is perhaps one piece we can take from this little line of scripture. Going just a bit deeper and stepping back from good things from time to time may in fact give us a greater appreciation for them, but also make them just a bit more holy. In both cases, our hearts are drawn to the joyful expectation of pleasures beyond our present understanding.

— *Preparing Room* —

Is there a place of excess in your life? Is there a closet in your heart's home that is so full that it is hard to enjoy what was put there for joy in the first place? Where do the words "there is a time for everything" speak to you? Read through Ecclesiastes 3:1-8 and consider making a choice like Joseph's—making more time and more space for the gift of gratitude and the gift of holiness.

A Prayer

O Lord, who for our sake didst fast forty days and
forty nights: give us grace to use such abstinence,
that, our flesh being subdued to the Spirit, we may
ever obey thy godly motions in righteousness, and
true holiness, to thy honour and glory, who livest and
reignest with the Father and the Holy Ghost, one God,
world without end.
Amen.

—Thomas Cranmer, d. 1556
The First Sunday in Lent
Book of Common Prayer, 1549[35]

---

35 Counsell, 195.

Impossible Possibles

And now, your relative Elizabeth in her old age has also conceived a son; and this is the sixth month for her who was said to be barren. For nothing will be impossible with God.

—Luke 1:36–37

As is the case with physical gifts from God, it is also possible to have skewed and even opposing understandings of those gifts of God that seem to defy our physical world. One word we use for something that seems to happen outside of our day-to-day realm is miracle.

One view, held by many in our twenty-first-century world, is that miracles are a mythical hope. Should something miraculous appear, it is merely defying our current ability to comprehend something that can, in time and with study, be explained with hard facts. Another view would believe that God is a kind of genie in a bottle. Rub the lamp enough with prayers, fasting, begging, and righteous living, and God will grant your wish—whether that be a parking place in front of the mall or an unexpected boost to your bank account. I would suggest that Christianity would not support either of these views.

For the record, I believe in miracles. I believe in slow ones that happen every day. The sunrise, sunset, and the orbiting planets in our solar system are, even with explanation, still a miracle in my mind. The journey from conception to birth is a miracle. Have you witnessed a birth? Can you really suggest there is not something miraculous there? As John Claypool used to say, "God is always changing water to wine . . . from fertile ground, well-planted seed, rain and sun come together to create grape, which under the right circumstances will in time, become wine to please the tongue and belly . . . we may understand it better . . . but it is still a miracle."[36]

I also believe in the miracles that seem, well, miraculous. Why doubt that the God who created the cosmos could not also separate the seas? Change a few fish and loaves to a feast? Walk on water or rise from the dead? Some believe in miracles, but believe they are about getting one's personal wish. Instead, all miracles, whether painted in brush strokes across pages of scripture, or encountered in daily life, have one aim: to point back to the Giver of all miracles.

Sometimes miracles seem very personal, almost as if God is playing favorites. As a priest, I have prayed with those who seem to be healed, and those whose healing came only when a sickness ended in death. Did God not hear the prayers? Or did God accord a miracle that was simply a reminder that sometimes and in some places God pokes his finger into our world as a way of pointing back to God, and thus reminding us of our deep need of him?

A lot has been placed before Mary up to the moment of her agreement to God's offer. Even with the personal visit from Gabriel, even with Gabriel's explanation of how it will all happen, she might have still been wondering what was up, or wondering whether it was all just a figment of her imagination.

Gabriel pushes the envelope. He tells Mary that her relative, Elizabeth, is also with child even though she is old and thought to have been barren. In our day, it is not unusual for an older woman to conceive even when she is thought to be barren. Luke has already introduced his reader to the genesis of this pregnancy as the opener to his Gospel.[37] But again, God's point is not to "razzle dazzle" Mary, but to fulfill God's purposes in and through her. The miracle that occurred in and through Elizabeth was merely to let Mary know that, if she was up for it, the same could happen in and through her.

---

36 This quote was taken from personal notes kept throughout the author's ministry.
37 Luke 1:5–25.

Miracles were spilling out all around: Elizabeth and her pregnancy, Gabriel's appearance to Mary and Joseph, and the promised coming Messiah, but all of them were not about a particular favorite. Instead, they were a reminder that all of God's children are equally loved. God wanted to show his miraculous love.

In my office, I keep a full-sized copy of a famous drawing by Leonardo da Vinci. It has been titled, "The Virgin and Child with

St. Anne and St. John the Baptist." The drawing shows four different biblical figures: Mary; Jesus; Mary's mother, Anne; and Elizabeth's child, John, who became the Baptist and paved the way for our Lord's ministry.[38]

While Mary's eyes are clearly fixed on her son playing with the child John, we see Anne, turning her gaze toward Mary, while pointing heavenward as if to say, "We are looking on two miracles from the One who has given them both to us."

Gabriel's balm to whatever was holding Mary back from the miracle that was about to begin was simply to say, "Mary, with God all things are possible." Embracing that reminds us that when God's plans are part of whatever drama may be unfolding before us, what may have seemed impossible begins to melt into the possible.

What miracle is God trying to accomplish in and through you? If you have even an inkling that it may be of God, then why doubt? Even if you do doubt, why not give it a try? Why not lay open your heart and risk making the impossible possible?

— *Preparing Room* —

Take some time today to wipe the doubt of impossible from the blackboard of your mind's eye. What miracles do you witness today? Write them down. Having witnessed those that are before you every day, take the next step and begin to partner with God. Knowing that with God all things are possible, then that means those things that are without Him seem impossible.

---

38 Luke 1:57–66, 3:1–22.

A Prayer

God eternal, all that is hidden is known to you,
All that will come to pass you see before it happens;
It is not your will that sinners should die:
You want them to repent and be saved.
Look, then, on this poor thing,
Pitiful, sinful, your servant.
May none of God's wonderful works
Keep silence, night or morning.
Bright stars, high mountains, the depths of the seas,
Sources of rushing rivers:
May all these break into song as we sing
To Father, Son and Holy Spirit.
May all the angels in the heavens reply:
Amen! Amen! Amen!
Power, praise, honour, eternal glory
To God, the only Giver of Grace.
Amen! Amen! Amen!

—A Prayer of the Third or Fourth Century CE
Found on Papyrus in the Dry Egyptian Desert[39]

---

39 Adalbert G. Hamman, comp. *Early Christian Prayers* (Chicago: H. Regnery Co., 1961), 68.

Let It Be . . .

Then Mary said, "Here am I, the servant of the Lord;
let it be with me according to your word." Then the
angel departed from her.

—Luke 1:38

After all the build-up, the dreams, the struggles, the fears, the
unanswered questions, Mary stands back, submits, and hum-
bles herself. The phrase alone spells out something movers and
shakers in the modern twenty-first century rarely hold in high
regard—humility. Of course, humility is a good thing as long as
it is Gandhi or Mother Teresa. In our fast-paced, success-oriented
world, the word humility is rarely pushed to the front of the "how
to be a success" story in your local grocery store rag.

Once Mary hurdles past her initial fears into a soft landing of
faith, she gives way to getting herself out of the way. With the
words, "Let it be," she acknowledges her role in what is about to
be the fulcrum of human history; a role that is not center stage,
but stage-hand.

Theologians sometimes call Mary the *Theotokos*, meaning
"God-bearer." She is the God-bearer, not God. In order for God
to do his work, God did not choose a rising star; God chose a servant. I actually like the King James Version of this passage where
Mary says, "Behold, I am the handmaid of the Lord." She got herself out of the way and that made all the difference.

What can we learn from Mary's humility? My hunch is that
Mary would not give a nod of approval to the movement we have
seen in the Church for many years called Marian devotion. She
might wince at being called "the blessed virgin" because, while

she recognized her blessing, she also knew it came from the outside in and not the inside out. We know that after Jesus's birth, she and Joseph offered the good Lord some sibling rivalry in children born after Jesus, thus the virginity was short-lived. She would not like to be portrayed in gold plate, or to be prayed to, or honored, or worshiped. My guess is that if you were praying in her presence and looked to her, she would not look back. She would have been looking up, pointing to the One to whom she not only gave life, but to whom she gave her life.

For that reason, and for her humility, we hold Mary in great devotion. We may call her blessed, but she certainly would not have done so. Mary was about Jesus, not the other way around.

In some instances, it has gotten downright ridiculous. Do you remember in 2004 when Diana Duyser said her ten-year-old's grilled cheese sandwich bore the image of Mary? It sold for $28,000 to an online casino business. Before she sold it, Duyser said, "I would like all people to know that I do believe that is the Virgin Mary Mother of God." Once she discovered it, she put it in a clear plastic box with cotton balls and kept it by her bed on her nightstand—until she sold it. I do not believe that is what Mary had in mind.

What we can learn from Mary's humility is the necessity of our own. Humility does not mean thinking ourselves unworthy; we are most worthy and favored in God's eyes. Frankly, that is what the whole story of God coming to be in our midst is about: God's love for and devotion to you.

Humility does mean putting ourselves in our places. Perhaps we would do well to print on the bottom of all mirrors, "Image may appear larger than it actually is." Mary knew enough to step aside from her dreams and visions to embrace what God wanted from her.

Time and time again, the path Jesus took was one of servitude. He lived by two words: you first. He displayed vertical humility before God and horizontal humility before others. And that was why Mary "found favor" with God; she was humble. If we want God to birth things in us, we too must be humble. We must be willing to step aside from ourselves and put our love of God and others before our own desperate needs and wants. When we do, we get to witness the birth of God right in our midst; we become exactly the kind of person God calls us to be.

When we do not find humility in our daily and spiritual lives, we then rely so very much on ourselves. And when we fail, well, then we find ourselves often in times of trouble, times of darkness. And thus, what is Mary's counsel? Turn our selfishness on its head. Turn from self-sufficiency to selflessness. Turn from what you want to what God may want for you. In other words, learn from Mary to pray a very, very powerful prayer . . . "Let it be, Let it be."

— *Preparing Room* —

Spend some time thinking on just one area of your life where you are wrestling with God—where you know God desires that you let him have the reins. What is holding you back from uttering Mary's prayer of submission, "Let it be"?

A Prayer

Incline us, O God, to think humbly of ourselves, to be saved only in the examination of our own conduct, to consider our fellow-creatures with kindness, and to judge of all they say and do with the clarity which we would desire from them ourselves; through Jesus Christ our Lord. *Amen.*

—Jane Austen, d. 1817[40]

---

40 Counsell, 341.

Relatively Speaking

In those days Mary set out and went with haste to a Judean town in the hill country, where she entered the house of Zechariah and greeted Elizabeth. When Elizabeth heard Mary's greeting, the child leaped in her womb. And Elizabeth was filled with the Holy Spirit and exclaimed with a loud cry, "Blessed are you among women, and blessed is the fruit of your womb. And why has this happened to me, that the mother of my Lord comes to me? For as soon as I heard the sound of your greeting, the child in my womb leaped for joy. And blessed is she who believed that there would be a fulfillment of what was spoken to her by the Lord."

—Luke 1:39–45

At this juncture miracles are underway. A miracle is making his way in and through Elizabeth's womb while a miracle is making his way in and through Mary's womb. Without looking back and without looking ahead, this is simply a moment of celebration and thanksgiving of what God has done for both of these women and of God's presence in their midst. The thanksgiving is so very powerful that it spills over into the babe in Elizabeth's womb who does his own little leap of joy. But perhaps beyond the celebration and thanksgiving comes a sound endorsement—a word of blessing from Mary's relative, Elizabeth.

Let us consider relatives. No one would argue that the world in which we live is far less connected than the one of our forebears perhaps only a century ago. There was a time when families were more connected. Children tended to settle close to home and the extended family was only a definition of relationship, not geography. Some would argue the distance that separates family might be a blessing, but such distance also tends to separate us from an appreciation of our forebears and all of our relatives for that matter. Part of growing into who we are called to be is embracing all of who we are. As I suggested in the opening meditation on Generations, we are who we are in part because of those from whom we came.

I have a friend who likes to joke that her favorite relative is her husband. "Because," she says, "I actually got to choose him." We do not get to choose our siblings, aunts, uncles, cousins, parents, or children. They are given to us by circumstances, by choices others make, by fate, and by God.

No one reading these words has a perfect family. Many reading these words have relatives who have not been a blessing. Instead they have been a burden and, in some cases, even a curse. But such relatives are still—welcomed or not—part of the makeup of who we are. These relatives speak to who we are whether we like it or not.

I have had both the blessing and the curse. There are those who have brushed up against my life who have left more scars than comforts, and those who have been more blessing than I could have ever imagined. Some of them were very close to me, some very distant, and some were in between. In all cases, I was related to them and they to me.

Understanding and embracing all the ways our relatives speak to us is an important piece of spiritual, emotional, and mental maturity. We must let our relatives (past and present) "speak" to us, help us understand better who we are. A distant parent may impede our ability to be an affectionate parent. It is best to deal with that wounded past so it can be healed as we move into the future. A loving relationship with a grandparent may remind us of the blessing of all relationships and how precious they are as our days with them are limited. The bond of a sibling can be a model for teaching our children how to love one another.

Just for clarification, understanding and embracing do not nec-essarily mean welcoming a destructive relationship into our lives. There are times when even relatives who have sorely wounded us must be kept at arm's length. Even then, the relative is speaking about what it means to turn from self to other. In the case between Mary and Elizabeth, the word spoken between them, the word leaping in Elizabeth's womb, the blessing of Elizabeth in the moment was a good word indeed. No doubt the love between these relatives bound them together in a way that showed generations to come how much joy there can be when hope, celebration, and love is shared.

— *Preparing Room* —

Spend some time thinking on those relatives who have cluttered your heart with pain or wounds or shame. Now embrace those relatives as a part of who you are and ask God to teach you from the hurt they have inflicted. Then clear your heart of what keeps you from the person God is calling you to be.

Now spend some time thinking on those relatives who have blessed you with friendship, joy, and love. Take the time needed to bask in the gifts they have offered you. Then ask God to let the word spoken to you, through them, be a blessing. That you, buoyed by their relationship, may live more fully into the person God is calling you to be.

A Prayer

God of all families and children,
God of all husbands and wives,
God of all daughters and sons,
God of all uncles and aunts,
God of Adam and Eve,
  Abraham and Sarah,
    Isaac and Rebekah,
      Jacob and Leah,
God of Joseph and Mary,
  Of the Prophets of Old and
    The Apostles of New,
God of saint and sinner alike,
  Of all the broken and all the whole,
God of my past,
  Of my now . . .
    Of my yet to be . . .
Help me to know that you seek to gather me under
the wings of Your care,
  As a mother hen gathers her chicks, with all those
  you have
    called into being, and
That trusting in Your never-failing love,
  I may have courage to embrace all that has been . . .
    To welcome all that is . . .
      And to fear not what has yet to come . . .
        Nor any you may send my way.
Amen.

Magnifying Glass

And Mary said, "My soul magnifies the Lord, and my spirit rejoices in God my Savior, for he has looked with favor on the lowliness of his servant. Surely, from now on all generations will call me blessed; for the Mighty One has done great things for me, and holy is his name. His mercy is for those who fear him from generation to generation.

He has shown strength with his arm; he has scattered the proud in the thoughts of their hearts. He has brought down the powerful from their thrones, and lifted up the lowly; he has filled the hungry with good things, and sent the rich away empty. He has helped his servant Israel, in remembrance of his mercy, according to the promise he made to our ancestors, to Abraham and to his descendants forever." And Mary remained with her about three months and then returned to her home.

—Luke 1:46–56

This passage is often called the Song of Mary and has been put to music in several ways over the years. It is a beautiful passage. One would do well to meditate and reflect on it alone throughout the Advent season.

It may seem contradictory to the passage in the meditation before last on Mary's humility. At first glance, some may think that Mary has sidestepped being humble. In a few lines, Mary sings about being favored: how God has done great things for her and how generation upon generation will look to her as "blessed."

Is Mary holding up a mirror or is she holding up a magnifying glass?

In the opening salvo Mary sings, "My soul magnifies the Lord." She does not say, "I am magnified," but, "My soul magnifies." In other words, her humility before God's call on her life has indeed caused her to be favored, to have great things done for her, and to be blessed.

Humility is one thing, submission is another. Mary's willingness to stand aside (humility) has resulted in her now being with child (submission). It is sometimes said that attitude determines altitude; in this case, Mary's lowliness was cause for her being lifted up.

Humility is knowing our place, while submission is taking our place. Humility is the starting point of knowing and opening ourselves up to what God may want to do in and through us. However, submission is going just a bit further. It is one thing to tell the doctor we are ready for the injection; it is another when we pull away as they come at us with the syringe. But Mary did both. She welcomed—"Let it be"—and then received the child—"My soul magnifies . . . ." Because she welcomed and received what was and continues to be, through her story we see magnification. Magnification, though not of Mary, but of God and all of God's qualities—mercy, strength, and justice.

As a child I often played with magnifying glasses. I liked to put them over a plant or an insect and move the glass back and forth. The ant's tiny antenna reminded me of tree branches, and the veins in leaves became like rivers running through a desert. I could better see what things really looked like by holding up the magnifying glass.

Mary, in her beautiful song, does not say, "Hey! Look at me!" but instead, "Look through me as if I were a magnifying glass showing you how great God is and what great things God can do." It is a reminder of the lengths to which God continues to go to show love to his children. We sometimes forget that.

Archbishop Desmond Tutu and his daughter, Mpho, who is also a priest, help us through this:

Sometimes it can be hard to see ourselves as God sees us. It can be impossible to imagine God's loving gaze. Maybe you don't recall ever being looked at lovingly. Perhaps you experience every gaze as critical, judgmental, disapproving, or, at best, indifferent. But that is not how God looks at us. God's gaze is like the gaze between lovers wrapped in a tender embrace. God looks at us the way a mother looks lovingly at her newborn baby. If you can see the loving gaze between mother and child in your mind's eye, you can begin a small meditation on being held in God's loving gaze. Once you are able to fix the gaze in your mind, put yourself in the sight line of the one gazing. Allow yourself to be the subject of that long, loving look. In this way you can imagine, then experience, the loving gaze that God turns to us. As we allow ourselves to accept God's acceptance, we can begin to accept our own goodness and beauty. With each glimpse of our own beauty we can begin to see the goodness and beauty in others.[41]

Mary could best see God by humbling herself before God. She could magnify God's love for all humanity by actually following her humility with her submission. With the marriage of humility and submission, Mary could see God's love for her and that same love for all of us is magnified through her. Now that is a magnifying glass not only worth holding, but looking through as well.

---

41 Desmond Tutu and Mpho Tutu, *Made for Goodness* (New York: HarperOne, 2010), 198.

— *Preparing Room* —

How are you called to actually submit to our Lord? If you have noted your station before God, what holds you back from allowing God to magnify himself through you now?

A Prayer

Give me vision, Oh Lord,
  To see me as Thou dost see me . . .
Give me submission, Oh Lord,
  To receive the love Thou dost have for me . . .
In that vision . . . in that giving way,
  May my soul be made new, and whole and full . . .
That I may love as Thou dost love,
  And magnify Thee . . .
  And all Thy ways . . .
Amen.

Circumstantial Evidence

In those days a decree went out from Emperor Augustus that all the world should be registered. This was the first registration and was taken while Quirinius was governor of Syria. All went to their own towns to be registered. Joseph also went from the town of Nazareth in Galilee to Judea, to the city of David called Bethlehem, because he was descended from the house and family of David. He went to be registered with Mary, to whom he was engaged and who was expecting a child. While they were there, the time came for her to deliver her child.

—Luke 2:1–6

Are you a fan of courtroom dramas? I am for a multitude of reasons. One is to see how cases are built upon evidence. Sometimes, what is offered in the way of evidence is circumstantial. In other words, there are no fingerprints, no weapon, no clear paper trail, just a set of circumstances that tend to point in one direction.

When the time comes for the baby Jesus to be born, all the events leading up to this moment come to a point of fruition, but there is no clear evidence that any of it actually happened. Luke points to the historically documented decree of Emperor Augustus that was issued at a specific time and in a specific way. As far as seeing a photograph of Joseph and Mary or having paperwork which showed their travel itinerary, the name of the street where they finally stopped, or knowledge of the exact day that Mary began to feel labor, we have zero evidence that any of it happened. It is all circumstantial, all conjecture, all based upon stories passed on with little, if any, proof.

What can thus be our response to such evidence? As usual, and as is the case with much of the Christian faith, God has left that up to us. God offers us a gift called faith to embrace the evidence, but, like all gifts, it must be received.

As a pastor and priest, I sometimes have to chuckle when skeptics appear with articles about how pieces of the Advent/Christmas story are not and cannot be true. Frankly, evidence against the story we Christians hold so dear is about as circumstantial as the evidence in favor of the story.

How should we respond to this circumstantial evidence? There are two little roads I would like to suggest. The first road says, do not let the details sidetrack us from the story. This applies to much of the Judeo-Christian faith. Let me offer an example. I know many good Christians who get hung up on the facts around the story of Jonah. Could a man really survive being swallowed by a whale? If so, how did he take all those notes? For the record, the story is not about the whale. Actually, a whale is never mentioned, it is, instead, a "great fish."[42] Jonah is a story about a reluctant prophet called to evangelize a people he hated, but God loved. God introduces the great fish—perhaps a grouper or jewfish—to keep Jonah on task. Jonah eventually does the work God calls him to do. The people repent and the book ends with Jonah angry at God. They do not teach that in Vacation Bible School. For some, the evidence both for and against a fish swallowing a prophet has absolutely nothing to do with the overall story—God's enduring and steadfast love for all humankind, and the lengths God will go to win them back. The journey down the first road says do not let the details rob us of the underlying truths.

---

42 Jonah 1:17; 2:1, 10. Many scholars suggest that the Book of Jonah was not literally true, but actually a play or tale inspired by God to display a more important truth—the truth of God's love.

The second road is a journey of faith that requires the listener to take the story into the soul. Not blind faith, but informed faith. I like the way Elton Trueblood put it, "Faith is not belief without proof, but trust without reservation."[43] Faith, when activated, embraces truths that have sustained Christians for over two thousand years, and our Jewish forebears for thousands of years before Christ.

Faith is a gift.[44] With many gifts, there are times when they come in handy, and other times when we may put them on the shelf. However, for those who follow Christ, faith is a daily exercise of stepping more deeply into things that cannot always be proven. "The righteous," we are told in scripture, live by faith.[45] It is that daily practice of taking God's unseen hand, trusting, and entrusting ourselves into truths that cannot be so much proven as lived. In time, faith proves itself. As Philip Yancey has written, "Faith means trusting in advance what will only make sense in reverse."[46]

Let us review Luke's circumstantial evidence. We can certainly get tangled in the details and, if we choose, we can write it off as fiction. But would a mythical tale set in an actual time have been the cause of countless numbers of named and unnamed followers of the Christ Child? Would a parable or storybook scene have caused the faith of his followers to build ministries and houses of worship that have literally changed the world as we know it? Could it all be a hoax? Something that just makes us feel good when things go bump in the night? Perhaps. Then again, consider the circumstantial evidence.

---

43 Edward K. Rowell, *1001 Quotes, Illustrations, and Humorous Stories for Preachers, Teachers, and Writers* (Grand Rapids, MI: Baker Books, 2008), 65.

44 Mark 9:24; 1 Corinthians 12:9; Galatians 5:22.

45 Habakkuk 2:4; Romans 1:17.

46 Rowell, 66.

— *Preparing Room* —

Is it hard to take hold of the whole of the Advent story? What stands in the way? Are you hung up on the details? Have you stepped out in faith? Can you let the details go, trust in the unseen, and let what God is telling you, through Mary's yet unborn child, speak to the hunger of your heart? Can you?

A Prayer

Belief, O Lord,
Is often too hard . . .
  There is nothing
to see . . .
  And when pain, or doubt,
Anger or worry overtake
me . . .
  Then faith seems but a dream . . .
I want to believe, I do so want to believe . . .
  Will you, help my . . .
unbelief?
  So that in believing, I may . . .
See and live the life . . .
  You give.
Amen.

Smelly Truths

**And she gave birth to her firstborn son and wrapped
him in bands of cloth, and laid him in a manger.**

—Luke 2:7

I suggested earlier that we have sanitized much of the Advent story.
Do you have a crèche in your home? We have several. One is filled
with well-crafted resin figurines. Another is carefully carved and
neatly painted wooden sculptures, and we also have one that fits
all neatly together into one Christmas decoration that hangs on
our tree each year.

In each case, everyone looks clean, orderly, and tidy. All the
animals are well groomed. The hay looks soft and the light glows
dimly. That is often the scene that we hold in our minds. Is it not?

I sometimes wonder if we need a bit more authenticity in our
scenes. Feel the brisk winter wind causing Mary and Joseph to
shiver, or the blazing Middle Eastern heat pulling reams of per-
spiration from their brow. See Mary's mouth still slightly open
from the heavy breathing of labor and delivery without anes-
thesia. If there was hay, it would likely have been wet or at least
damp. It would have certainly been used by the creatures that
were salivating over it while they consumed it. Perhaps the animals were impatiently waiting for the little congregation to
leave so they could sleep where they always slept. And, if this
manger—the shabby little barn or small cave, as was sometimes
the case—was inhabited by animals, it was not the smell of cin-
namon, spice, and evergreen pines that welcomed Mary and her
new babe, but something much worse. And yet, that is what the
innkeeper offered. This was the only space he had. It was both a

place of comfort and discomfort, rest and restlessness, pain and pleasure, beginnings and endings, the sweet smell of hay and the disgusting smells that often lived among that hay.

Years ago I read an outstanding sermon by Episcopal priest, Barbara Brown Taylor who unpacked some thinking around this by focusing in on Mary. She was clear about saying that we should be on guard about taking away the "Mary-ness" of the Madonna because, in doing so, we may very well take away from the "Jesus-ness" of Christ. She went on to say that if we cut out the inevitable humiliation Mary had to have faced, being pregnant and unmarried in a small town, then we deny her anguish. If we presume that everyone else in Nazareth heard the same message Gabriel gave to Mary and that made the neighbors collectively supportive of her, we need to think again. If we remove the rigors of full-term pregnancy, insisting that Mary somehow did not have to endure morning sickness, varicose veins, hemorrhoids, or hormonal headaches, assuming that she just sailed into the manger nine months later without any natural realities, then we miss the power of Mary's witness. The Incarnation becomes the "incantation," something magical, ethereal, netherworldly, and, frankly, untrue.[47] The truth, the whole truth, is usually not as beautiful as it seems, but it is part of the truth. That cute bundle of joy behind the glass in the hospital was only hours before covered with blood and tissue that made that life possible. The full details of the story remind us of a very important truth—God meets us where we are. Is that good news to you?

What if God could only work in pure and stainless environments? What if our lives and hearts had to resemble sterile operating rooms before the Great Physician could get to work? No, God's work is more often done in places that are dark, damp, dirty, and disgusting. It is a smelly truth, but an important one because of what it plainly says: God takes all comers.

That beautiful passage in Matthew, "Come to me, all you that are weary and are carrying heavy burdens, and I will give you

---

47 This illustration was in my preaching notes from a sermon preached by Barbara Brown Taylor, but I apologize for not having a direct source..

rest" (11:28), says about as much about Jesus as anyone could want to know. Jesus does not say, "Come only if." He says, "Come," and the only qualification seems to be an invitation especially to those weary and burdened.

Hold on to the Madonna and hold on to the Christ. Do not let go of Mary, do not let go of Jesus. They have some smelly truths for us that are worth breathing in deeply.

— *Preparing Room* —

Take some time to meditate on the sights and smells that Mary and Joseph might have encountered in that manger—the smelly ones! How does knowing that God meets you where you are and does His work right in the midst of where you are, free up room in your heart for more of His love to invade you?

A Prayer

Since you came into the world for all people, O Saviour, therefore you came for me, for I am one of the people. Since you came into the world to save sinners, therefore you came to save me, for I am one of the sinners. Since you came to find those who are lost, therefore you came to find me, for I am one of the lost. O Lord, O my God and Creator! I should have come to you as a transgressor of your law. . . . But I was so proud and so stubborn that you had to come to me. You had to come down to earth as a tiny baby, enduring poverty, discomfort and danger, in order to reach me. You had to walk dusty lanes, enduring insults and persecution, in order to reach me. You had to suffer and die on a cross, in order to reach me. Forgive me my stubborn pride that I have put you to such trouble and such pain on my behalf . . . .

And thy mercy will follow me all the days of my life: so that, being preserved by your grace, I shall offer you thanksgiving, face to face, with your chosen ones, and shall sing, and praise, and glorify you, with the Eternal Father and the Holy Ghost, forever and ever. *Amen.*

—Tychon of Zadonsk, d. 1783[48]

48 Helen Iswolsky, trans., "Confession and Thanksgiving to Christ, Son of God, the Saviour of the Word," in *A Treasury of Russian Spirituality*, ed. G. P. Fedotov (New York: Sheed & Ward, 1948).

Room or No Room . . .
That Is the Question

. . . because there was no place for them in the inn.

—Luke 2:7

Poor innkeeper. He has been consistently bad-mouthed since Mary and Joseph's story came on the scene. The inn was full. Perhaps it was because everyone was coming in for Augustus's headcount. Maybe it was wedding season and he had the best bridal suites in town. Maybe he opened his door, saw a young man with a pregnant teenager sitting on a donkey, and he did not want any trouble. For whatever reason, he was not going to give up one of his suites to a couple who probably needed one more than anyone else, but while there may not have been a room, he did make room. And because he did, Jesus had a place to be born, Mary had a place to recover, and Joseph could offer a small sigh of relief.

As I referenced in the preface, I have called this little book *Preparing Room* for a reason. I love the hymn "Joy to the World," which is often sung on Christmas Day in Christian churches throughout the world. The words penned by Isaac Watts in 1719 are simplistically beautiful:

> Joy to the world, the Lord is come!
> Let earth receive her King;
> Let every heart prepare Him room![49]

---

49 *The Hymnal*, 100.

In order to prepare room, we have to make room. I know when we have guests in our home, my wife makes certain that the room is straight. She makes sure that there is room set aside for luggage, for hanging clothes, for shoes, and for anything else one might set down—a book, a Bible, a purse. In order to make room, less important things need to be moved away, sometimes even thrown away.

Watts's hymn is an announcement and invitation, then a directive. First, he announces "joy" to the entire world because the Lord of all creation has come. Second, he invites that same world to "receive" the King. And lastly, in order to receive that king, hearts must "prepare" room by setting aside a space for him— move things, throw things away.

Of course, no one can compel one to be joyful or recognize the Lord. No one can force another to receive this invitation or receive the King behind it. And no one can demand that a heart prepare room for this King. No, all of the words here are offerings and they can be received or rejected, welcomed or shunned.

We have the choice: to make room or not to make room? That is the question, to paraphrase Hamlet. Do we want joy? Do we want the King? Do we want Christ to take up residence in our hearts? Well, God has left that choice up to each of us.

The invitation to embrace the Advent story is a knock at the door. When we open it, and we see Joseph, Mary, and the Babe waiting to be born in us, how will we answer the question, "Room . . . or no room?"

— *Preparing Room* —

I have spent a great deal of time suggesting that you look at things that might take up space in your heart in a way that leaves no room for the Christ Child. As we start toward the end of our Advent meditations, I will push a bit more for this making room. But for now, what room needs to be made just today? What immediately comes to mind? Can you toss it aside? Can you make room in your heart for his birth in you?

A Prayer

Ah, dearest Jesus, Holy Child,
Make thee a bed, soft, undefiled,
Within my heart, that it may be
A quiet chamber kept for thee.
Welcome to earth, thou noble guest,
Through whom the wicked men are blest!
Thou com'st to share our misery,
What can we render, Lord to Thee!
Ah, Lord, who has created all,
How hast thou made thee weak and small,
That thou must choose thy infant bed
Where ass and ox but lately fed!
Were earth a thousand times as fair
Beset with gold and jewels rare,
She yet were far too poor to be,
A narrow cradle, Lord, for thee.
For velvets soft and silken stuff
Thou has but hay and straw so rough.
Whereon thou king, so rich and great.
As 'twere thy heaven, art throned in state.
Thus hath it pleased thee to make plain
The truth to us poor fools and vain.
That this world's honour, wealth and might
Are nought and worthless in thy sight . . .
Amen.

—Martin Luther, d. 1546[50]

---

[50] Martin Luther, "Vom Himmel Hoch," Catherine Winkworth, trans. in *2000 Years of Prayer,* Michael Counsell, comp. (Harrisburg, PA: Morehouse, 1999), 180–81.

God's Angle on Shepherds

In that region there were shepherds living in the fields, keeping watch over their flock by night. Then an angel of the Lord stood before them, and the glory of the Lord shone around them, and they were terrified. But the angel said to them, "Do not be afraid; for see—I am bringing you good news of great joy for all the people: to you is born this day in the city of David a Savior, who is the Messiah, the Lord."

—Luke 2:8–11

For virtually all the years of my ordained ministry, I have served parishes with schools. Some had middle schools and primary schools, but all had pre-schools. The Advent season is undoubtedly craft time in parochial schools. Often little "packages" have been delivered to my office by teachers proud of the theological insights of their youngsters. When these packages are sound, deep, and meaningful, they bring a smile to the face and heart. Such is the case when I have received the nativity scene with each character identified—and on more than one occasion, fluttering above the manger has been one of God's angels.

But as I have thought of the spiritual errand boys of God, it strikes me that an angel's real job is to bring clarity to a particular story. God's angels are often sent into the story to give God's angle.

A moment of biblical clarity here—it is not uncommon to believe that when we cross the veil between death to life, we are given wings and granted angelic status, or that we arrive and then have to earn our wings. Scripture counters such claims.

Angels are different kinds of creatures from humans. We may know humans who possess angelic qualities, or have even seen babies cute as cherubs fluttering in the clouds. But scripture teaches angels were actually around before humans and that they are given specific duties. Announcing news is one of those duties.[51]

Here, the news is very good. We do not know everyone to whom the angels appeared that night to share the good news, but we know that the shepherds were among them. Shepherds were an important cog in the ancient agricultural wheel. Sheep and goats provided multiple goods, from milk and cheese, to heartier food and even clothing. Shepherds were scattered all over the countryside, so obviously it was a good choice to tell a shepherd, who would tell another, who would tell another, and so on.

But shepherds also became a kind of forebearer of the Christ Child. "I am the good shepherd," Jesus said. "I know my own and my own know me. . . . I lay down my life for the sheep."[52] For a moment here, we see a little dance of sorts between two important groups. First, God's angels drop in to make sure everyone is clued in on the story, that everyone has God's angle. And then we have God's shepherds, whom Jesus would choose to tell another part of the story. Jesus's coming was not just about a babe in the manger, but a protector in the darkness who, when the time comes, would lay down his life for his sheep—that would be you and me.

In this part of the story at least, God is using angels and shepherds as important players in a rather large drama that spells out some very good news: God loves you.

---

51 Genesis 16:7, 22:11; Exodus 23:20; Judges 6:22; 1 Kings 19:7; Hosea 12:4; Matthew 2:13; Luke 22:43; Acts 12:7; Hebrews 2:7; Jude 6.
52 John 10:14–15.

— *Preparing Room* —

If God's angle is to have you understand God's great love for you, a love so great that in his Son, he would lay down his life for you, then what pieces of this story speak to you? Is it the angel sent on special assignment? Is it the angel's word to "not be afraid"? Is it the joy, the birth, the shepherd? Pick one or two words in the story and let them usher into your heart just a bit more of that very good news of God's love.

A Prayer

That you would come and live and die for me?
To show your love, remove my sin?
That you would lay aside your crown for me, dear Lord?
Is all too, too much to take in.
That you have sent angels to announce?
And given Shepherds to display?
Awakens my heart and soul,
Takes my breath away.
Silence me, O Lord, and
Still my rapid pace,
That my soul may receive you yet
And I end my restless race.
Give me, I pray, a heart
That welcomes you.
Give me, I pray, a soul
That is renewed.
Amen.

Signs

"This will be a sign for you: you will find a child wrapped in bands of cloth and lying in a manger." And suddenly there was with the angel a multitude of the heavenly host, praising God and saying, "Glory to God in the highest Heaven, And on earth peace among Those whom he favors!" When the angels had left them and gone into heaven, the shepherds said to one another, "Let us go now to Bethlehem and see this thing that has taken place, which the Lord has made known to us."

—Luke 2:12–15

Some years ago, M. Night Shyamalan produced a movie entitled *Signs*. On the surface, it was an alien/science fiction film where mysterious crop circles served as signs that pointed the way for safe landings of alien spacecraft. Below the surface, however, were myriad signs that sprang to life around the story of an Episcopal priest who had given up his collar when his wife was tragically killed in an accident. I will let you find out what happens from there, but it is not until the end of the film that one realizes how many signs there were that pointed to a way out of the clergyman's misery.

There are a good many signs that start popping up at this point in the Advent story. Angels surfaced in our last meditation, a star will emerge, and the shepherds will confirm what the angels had told them by finding the child wrapped up in bands of cloth and lying in a manger. As we follow the shepherds as they head into town, sheep in tow, looking for a manger and listening for a baby, check out his clothes when they find him. If they match the description, then the sign confirms the messages of God.

Signs are important. I once lived along the Gulf and came to enjoy blue crabs. If the "Live Blue Crab" sign was lit at my favorite fish market, I knew it was time to stop in and collect my share. Same goes for the Krispy Kreme "Hot Doughnuts Now" sign.

Signs not only invite us; they warn us too—like the three primary traffic signs: Stop, Wrong Way, and Yield. Stop signs are there for obvious reasons. They are there to protect us, allow us to pause, and even save our lives. A Stop sign at an intersection can keep us from being pummeled by an eighteen-wheeler.

Our lives are full of Stop signs. We are moving in one direction and all is going well and then something changes it all: job loss, an unexpected report from the doctor, divorce papers, a hurricane, the death of a friend. These make us stop and consider our own lives. Are we using or abusing our lives?

The events around Jesus's birth comprise one of God's Stop signs. It was as though God was saying, "It is time to put things right, so everyone hold on a minute and pay attention." That is the reason for the prophecies. That is the reason for the virgin, the star, the angels, and so on. This birth was like no other. God used these signs to say "STOP!"

And this Stop sign was the beginning of Christian understanding of the redemption of humankind. The great Church father,

Athanasius of Alexandria, once wrote, "Christ became what we are that He might make us what He is." This Stop sign is the place where we begin to consider how all the bad things can be put in order and all the wrong ways can be turned right.

That is where the Wrong Way sign comes in. I have, on more than one occasion, accidently gone the wrong direction on a one-way street. Somewhere, I missed a prominently displayed

Wrong Way sign and put my life in danger. Wrong Way signs are there for a reason. They tell us that we are obviously going the wrong way. Jesus sent several of them. These signs were sprinkled among his teachings, miracles, and admonitions.

Jesus said a lot of lovely things, but we also need to remember that the first word we have recorded of his public ministry was simple: *repent*.[53] It was not *love, follow,* or *include,* but *repent*—because Jesus knew that if we did not start by getting the yuck out of our lives, we would never get the love, follow, and include business right.

Part of my ministry over the years has been to hold up Wrong Way signs to people—not necessarily in a judgmental or harsh way, but to bring clarity. Clarity to the wife who is being unfaithful to her husband, the child who is caught in a web of drugs, the executive who cannot turn loose the bottle, or the parent who cannot let go of their anger. The point of the Wrong Way sign is to encourage humanity to repent, stop going in the wrong direction, and instead take the right way to life, health, wholeness, and salvation.

Over the years, I have had people close to me hold up Wrong Way signs when I did not see disaster coming. Sometimes I heeded the warning; sometimes I did not. If there is something that is crippling our daily lives or, worse yet, destroying our souls, Jesus's word *repent* should be a welcome sign that turns us around in a much better direction.

Now an important part of letting the Stop sign and the Wrong Way sign work is to follow the Yield sign. Yield signs can be a bit awkward. You're left wondering, "Who goes first?" "How long do I wait?" The British have a sign that is a bit more direct: Give Way. To yield means to give way. In its fullness it means we are not first in line, but last. It means we have to put ourselves aside and let someone else go before us. If everyone went first, then there would not be enough patrolmen on the streets to take care of all the accidents.

The need to yield is essential in the Christian life. As Christians, when we are encouraged to yield, it means essentially to let go—to

---

53 Matthew 4:17.

rest our faith in Christ. In order to observe God's Stop sign, we have to yield to God's command; the same goes for the Wrong Way sign. These signs are all important because they are pointing in the same direction back to God. Back to the redemption, hope, and finally salvation offered in Christ.

In the last line of the movie *Signs*, Morgan, the son of the doubting priest Graham, is brought back from the brink of death after his father's heartfelt and anguished prayer to God. As he clutches his son in tears, the boy looks up and says, "Did someone save me?" Graham realizes at that moment what is going on and he says, "Yeah, baby, I think someone did."

Someone wants to save us, too. And it is precisely because of God's love for us that God sends signs all the time: Stop, Wrong Way, Yield. These signs are there to help you, heal you, save you. Well?

— *Preparing Room* —

What signs has God placed before you in recent days? Are you paying attention to them? Are you yielding to their protection? If not, why? If so, then where will you go next?

A Prayer

I ask you, by the power of your most sweet name, and by your holy manhood's mystery, to put away my sins and heal the languors of my soul, mindful only of your goodness, not of my ingratitude. Lord, may your good, sweet Spirit descend into my heart, and fashion there a dwelling for himself. *Amen.*

—Aelred of Rievaulx, d. 1167[54]

---

54 Sister Rose de Lima, trans., "For Crist luve: Prayers of St. Aelred" in *2000 Years of Prayer*, Michael Counsell, comp. (Harrisburg, PA: Morehouse, 1999), 118.

Treasure Chest

So they went with haste and found Mary and Joseph, and the child lying in the manger. When they saw this, they made known what had been told them about this child; and all who heard it were amazed at what the shepherds told them. But Mary treasured all these words and pondered them in her heart. The shepherds returned, glorifying and praising God for all they had heard and seen, as it had been told them.

—Luke 2:16–20

Luke's orderly telling of the Advent and Christmas story ends by pointing to the culmination of all the events leading up to the birth of Jesus, and climaxing with the visit of the shepherds who only confirm what Mary had been told by Gabriel.

We are told that when Mary heard it all, she "treasured all these words, and pondered them in her heart." Mary treasured the words because they were confirmation of what had been promised. It was the fruit of a miraculous conception, months of labor, and, finally, delivery of God in human form. What we do not know is what Mary specifically pondered in her heart. I believe Mary pondered the gift of life.

Much of the heartache I have experienced and witnessed in my ministry has been from the fruit of ingratitude. I have been guilty of it and have witnessed what such ingratitude does in the lives of others. Perhaps it is human nature to notice who is ahead and who is behind; who has more or less; who is attractive, wealthy, or successful and who is not. This constant comparison between your life and possessions with those of others is something I like to call "comparative living." I think our media-driven world has made comparative living worse. Television, magazine covers, or a quick internet search can quickly lead us to that person who is just one rung above us on life's ladder. And if we spend much time investing in this comparative living, we will lose the game of "one-up-man-ship" because we can always find someone who seems to have it better than we do. What about appreciating what we have and where we are right now? What about enjoying the time we have been given and the relationships and work God has entrusted to us? Can you appreciate the moment we are in right now?

The truth is that comparative living can work both ways. Whether looking up or down the ladder, we will always find someone doing better or worse than we are. This downward and upward gaze keeps your eyes and our heart from missing the rung we have been asked to hold. How can we accept the invitation to "be content with what we have"?[55]

No one taught me this better than John Claypool. John had witnessed much heartache in his many years of pastoral ministry, but none as difficult as the heartache he felt when his daughter's life gave way after a lengthy battle with childhood leukemia. I remember John telling me that, though he knew her death was imminent, when she took her last breath, he could not believe it; he was overwhelmed with grief. Some days after her death, John took his wife and son to the restaurant they always visited on Sundays after church. He said they sat in their favorite spot and his eyes turned to her empty chair. It was at that moment when he thought, "I just do not know how I can go on."

Then, almost as a gift of grace, his eyes fell on his son and his heart turned. He thought, "I have to go on; there is my son whom I love as much as my daughter and who needs me now more than ever." It was the beginning of a process that ultimately guided John to a monumental decision about moving through the valley of the shadow of death. John contemplated in his heart that he could spend the rest of his life being angry at God and the world

---

55 Hebrews 13:5.

because his daughter left this life after only ten years, or he could spend the rest of his life being thankful that he ever had her in his life at all. He chose gratitude for the life entrusted to his care. It was then that John had his favorite motto, "Life is a Gift" engraved on a little plaque and displayed on his desk.

A treasure chest is a place where one usually stores things of great value. Mary chose her heart as her "treasure chest." She pondered not what laid ahead for her new babe, but the moment itself, the child himself. My guess is she did not think, "I wish this was just my baby and not God's," or "I wish we were not in this smelly manger," or "How on earth did these shepherds find out and what are they doing here?" My hunch is, she just took it all in and gave thanks for the gift of life and treasured that in her heart. A treasure chest indeed. We would be wise to do the same for every minute we have been given.

— *Preparing Room* —

Where do you find yourself comparing your life to the lives of others? Ponder the waste of time that may be, and then make room in your heart for the gift of life you have been given. Can you?

A Prayer

The following is not a written prayer, but a body prayer taught to me years ago by John Claypool. Take a moment and stand. Place your hands by your sides and in your mind's eye, physically gather all the pain, anxiety, sin, worry, and fear you may carry with you. Now, by literally moving your hands from your sides up to your heart, collect these cares as you move your hands to your heart.

Once your hands reach your heart, hold them there for just a moment. Then take them in your hands and move your hands upward, forming your arms into a chalice and offering these parts of your soul to God's redeeming grace. Leave your hands there for a moment; release them all.

Now leaving your hands and arms open as a chalice, again in your mind's eye, envision God pouring His healing, grace, forgiveness, life, and peace into your arms. Once you have received them, move your hands and arms back down, placing these gifts into your heart. Hold your hands there for a moment, and then move them slowly to your sides, allowing those gifts to then pour out of your heart into the rest of your being.

Stand meditating on these gifts and end with the words, "I receive, in Jesus's name, *Amen*."

Wisdom of the Ages

In the time of King Herod, after Jesus was born in Bethlehem of Judea, wise men from the East came to Jerusalem, asking, "Where is the child who has been born king of the Jews? For we observed his star at its rising, and have come to pay him homage." When King Herod heard this, he was frightened, and all Jerusalem with him; and calling together all the chief priests and scribes of the people, he inquired of them where the Messiah was to be born. They told him, "In Bethlehem of Judea; for so it has been written by the prophet: 'And you, Bethlehem, in the land of Judah, are by no means least among the rulers of Judah; for from you shall come a ruler who is to shepherd my people Israel.'"[56]

—Matthew 2:1–6

For whatever reason, only Matthew introduces us to the wise men from the East. An important piece of Matthew's writing was to clearly link Jesus's coming as the Messiah of the Jews. He begins his story with Jesus's birth in David's city, Bethlehem. It is interesting to note that there was another city by the name of Bethlehem, roughly seven miles northwest of Nazareth. Matthew writes "Bethlehem of Judea" to stress that Jesus came from the same people and area as the davidic kings.

Let me touch once more on humility. We are told that once Jesus was born, wise men came asking where to find him. Some

---

56 Micah 5:2.

interpretations suggest that the men were a mix of astronomers (those who studied the stars) and astrologers (those who read signs in the stars). Whatever the case, the "star" itself was an announcement that something big had occurred. It was more expansive than the wisdom of the wise, or Herod's fear, and bigger than the power of the powerful.

The wise men clearly knew their scriptures, as they quoted the ancient prophet Micah. In order to step beyond what the announcing star meant, they had to draw not from their own wisdom, but from the wisdom of the ages. This necessitated humility before the Holy Scriptures in order to learn from them and discover such greatness. It brought the wise men excitement.

Pride we know is a tough pill to swallow. That means its antonymic quality, humility, must be equally as difficult to digest. During his ministry, Jesus taught, "All who exalt themselves will be humbled, but all who humble themselves will be exalted" (Luke 18:14). Humility is not a kind of quivering submission. Nor is it self-abasement that would devalue the love God has for us, or that we should have for ourselves. Instead, humility is usually a quality that springs to life out of our relationship with Christ. It is fruit from a well-planted tree. It is hard to try and be humble because, in doing so, one would likely slip into pride. An example of this might sound like, "Ah! Look at how humble I have become."

The very first Christian creed was not the Apostle's Creed, authored around 110 BCE, nor the Nicene Creed, authored in the year 325. The very first creed was simple, composed of three words: "Jesus is Lord." Ancient Christians who were ready for baptism were asked to proclaim this creed and, in doing so, were granted admission into the Christian family through the sacrament of baptism.

Recognizing Jesus as Lord has been done by princes and paupers, garbage collectors and presidents, scientists and train conductors. Humans of all ages, races, and nations recognize Him as such. But in order to call someone lord, there must be an element of humility; one must recognize that lord's authority. To call Jesus Lord is to recognize his ultimate authority over our lives. Such submission would mean when our lives bump up against that authority, the authority wins—no ifs, ands, or buts.

The wise men were ready to put aside their wisdom in favor of a greater wisdom. Here we see a hint of what Jesus's entire life would soon be about: the call to follow him as Lord and King. We have before us the choice to call him King and live our lives for him. Living with Christ as Lord means he is Lord of all of us—our work, leisure, possessions, relationships, morals, ethics.

We do, of course, struggle. There are days in my own life when it is clear as glass that Jesus is not Lord of every aspect of my life. That does not lessen or weaken the invitation to embrace his Lordship and take up the mantle of Christian living. But when we stumble and fall away from that Lordship, we return to him again, with that same humility that brought us to him in the first place.

One more point about humility and the Lordship of Christ. Virtually every good or great thing I ever learned, I learned from someone or something with more knowledge and wisdom than myself. Humility is an ongoing quality that leads to better or greater ways of living. Some may see humility as, well, humiliating. Humility could suggest one has restricted themselves to new parameters we might not have known before. Some would also suggest that to call Jesus "Lord" takes away our freedom to be our own lord.

But if heeding that call leads to a better life full of peace, spiritual health, and salvation, is that bondage or freedom? A road without guardrails next to a cliff may seem like real freedom until the car spins into the ravine. The "lordship" of the rails helps the car get to where it is going. To become who God created us to be by following Christ, means we are freer than we could ever be without his Lordship. This is precisely what the Apostle Paul meant when he wrote to the Christians in Corinth, "Now the Lord is the Spirit, and where the Spirit of the Lord is, there is freedom" (2 Corinthians 3:17).

The wise men began to find their way to their King by humbling themselves before the wisdom of the ages and gained more with every step toward him. One could, out of pride or fear, reject or run from that wisdom. That is precisely the path that Herod chose to take, and with that a dark cloud appears on the horizon of this wonderful story.

For now, let us consider the path of the wise men.

— *Preparing Room* —

Where in your own life have you gained by submitting to the wisdom of another? What, if any, part of your life resists the Lordship of Christ? What is holding you back from allowing that part to call Him Lord?

A Prayer

Guide us, O Lord, in all the changes and varieties of the world; that we may have evenness and tranquility of spirit: that we may not murmur in adversity nor in prosperity wax proud, but in serene faith resign our souls to thy divinest will; through Jesus Christ our Lord. *Amen.*

—Jeremy Taylor, d. 1667[57]

---

57 Counsell, 278.

Something Wicked This Way Comes

Then Herod secretly called for the wise men and learned from them the exact time when the star had appeared. Then he sent them to Bethlehem, saying, "Go and search diligently for the child; and when you have found him, bring me word so that I may also go and pay him homage."

—Matthew 2:7–8

In 1962, author Ray Bradbury wrote a fantasy/horror novel entitled *Something Wicked This Way Comes.* It opens with two teenage boys who are drawn into the net of a frightening traveling carnival that arrives in their town in the early autumn. The reader is soon introduced to the carnival's operator, Mr. Dark, and learns he has a tattoo for each human pulled into his ominous fantasies and under his control.

There is obviously more to the story, but suffice it to say, all seems well and good until the arrival of the carnival and Mr. Dark. Such is the case with the Advent story. Up to this point, the story has been beautiful, mystifying, exciting, and filled with wonder and hope. There have been some moments of fear and doubt, but those were ultimately wiped away with God's assurances about the full unfolding of the story.

But now we see things take a crooked turn. Unlike the wise men who are drawn to Jesus as King, Herod fears him as a threat. He secretly calls the wise men and, with a lie, launches a plan that will ultimately fail, but leads untold numbers of infant boys in Bethlehem to their deaths.[58] This part of the saga seems like a nasty and putrid wound on an otherwise healthy and strong body. But it is a wound that reminds us there is evil in the world.

Evil, as Christians understand it, has its birthplace in selfishness. The more we turn inward, the more we turn away from God and those whom God has called us to live among and serve. It was Herod's selfish desire that there be no threats to his little kingdom or his authority that caused him to seek the Christ Child and order the slaughter of the innocents. Notice how a selfish plan, a secret meeting, a so-called little white lie, all snowballed into the horror of infanticide. Herod wanted no lord. He alone wanted to be lord and that is precisely where the trouble began.

We live in a time, not uncommon from others, where even religious people have trouble with the concept of evil. The explanations for darkness that humans choose point to culture, parenting, socialization, and even nutrition. But, to defeat evil, we must first name it. The doctor does not heal an infection in the knee by treating a sore throat. If they are a good doctor, they diagnose the location and get to work on the place the infection began.

The Bible tells the story of evil across most of its pages. Jesus counseled against evil thoughts and actions, cast out evil spirits, and prayed that he might be "delivered from evil."[59] In one of his more startling sermons, Jesus said, "For all who do evil hate the light and do not come to the light, so that their deeds may not be exposed" (John 3:20). The remedy? Paul wrote to Christians living in an increasingly evil culture, "Hate what is evil, hold fast to what is good" (Romans 12:9), which means recognizing and naming evil when it is seen, turning from it, thereby defeating its power, and clinging to what is the ultimate good: God in Christ.

Do you doubt the existence of evil? Read the first few pages of your morning newspaper, watch the evening news, sit through a few hours of primetime television. Do they not whisper of those

---

58 Matthew 2:16–23.
59 Matthew 6:13, 17:18; Mark 7:21, 30.

who have chosen to try and be their own god? Wouldn't you agree that the stories we read and watch speak of those who foolishly attempt to run their own lives and only end up wreaking havoc on their lives and the lives of others?

Herod reminds us there is a force at work in the world that hates that which is good and righteous, pure and holy. It has but one goal: to keep the sheep of the Great Shepherd out of his care and protection. That is why it is so important to know evil and be able to say, "Something wicked this way comes." We cannot turn from evil if we do not believe in it or fail to see it. Like Herod, the worst evil sometimes starts small and simply builds until devastation occurs. We see this when a social habit transforms into an addiction, an innocent flirtation blossoms into infidelity, hard work shifts into blind ambition, and when a desire to serve becomes an obsession to rule.

An old story about a cowboy and a rattlesnake speaks to us about identifying and dealing with evil. The cowboy begins to bunk down for the night and a rattlesnake slides up next to his sleeping bag. At first the man is frightened, but the snake says, "Don't be frightened! I won't hurt you. But it is cold out here. Can I crawl into that sleeping bag with you for the night?"

"If you promise not to hurt me," says the cowboy.

"Oh I promise, I promise," replies the snake.

The cowboy picks up the snake, places him at the opening of the bag, and it slides in, sleeping near his feet, nice and warm throughout the night until morning.

When the cowboy awakes, he stretches, stands, and tells the snake, "Time to rise and shine," at which point the snake curls, rattles his little tale, and strikes, biting the man with poisonous fangs.

The cowboy cries, "What did you do that for? You promised you would not hurt me and now I am likely to lose my life."

The snake just smiles and whispers, "You knew what I was when you picked me up." Then he slithers away leaving the man to die.

If Herod had pondered his actions long enough, he might have realized where his slippery slope would lead. Have you stepped out onto any slippery slopes?

— *Preparing Room* —

Jesus once said, "For out of the heart come evil intentions."[60] That is a rather harsh indictment, but it is true. Is there anything in the rooms of your heart that needs to be named as evil? Dark? Sinful? Selfish? Can you turn it over to God in Christ as a confession, making more room for His grace, mercy, and love?

A Prayer

Most merciful God,
we confess that we have sinned against thee
in thought, word, and deed,
by what we have done,
and by what we have left undone.
We have not loved thee with our whole heart;
we have not loved our neighbors as ourselves.
We are truly sorry and we humbly repent.
For the sake of thy Son Jesus Christ,
have mercy on us and forgive us;
that we may delight in thy will,
and walk in thy ways,
to the glory of thy Name.
Amen.[61]

---

60 Matthew 15:19.
61 *The Book of Common Prayer* (New York: Church Hymnal Corporation, 1979), 331.

Star Power

When they had heard the king, they set out; and
there, ahead of them, went the star that they had
seen at its rising, until it stopped over the place
where the child was. When they saw that the star had
stopped, they were overwhelmed with joy.

—Matthew 2:9–10

About twice a year, at my request, my wife buys a copy of *People* magazine for me. Not to bash the magazine too much, but the reading is not heavy lifting. It is, however, filled with good sermon illustrations. I will leave that to your imagination.

If you have ever flipped through an issue, you will know that most of the articles and photos focus on the habits, lives, and work of those in the entertainment business—rock stars, television stars, and movie stars. One of the reasons I read the magazine is that part of me is fascinated at what constitutes "star power," and how that power is so elusive and fleeting. The person on the cover one week may be buried deep in the back of the next issue.

What is it that draws us to pay attention to the stars? What is it that draws some to want that star power? Any rational person knows such power can fade as quickly as the setting sun. We can learn from the wise men who, after encountering Herod, set out to follow a heavenly star. This star drew them to something—to Someone—who had a star power that was not earned, but given and would never fade away.

For Christians, there is but one core of our faith: Jesus Christ. The Apostle Paul, who authored most of the New Testament epistles, wrote on a wide variety of matters from theology and morality, to Church practice and evangelism. He gave us a little peek into the heart of his motivation when writing to the Christians at the church he founded in Corinth. Corinth was a seedy port town. It was a crossroads for ancient commerce and trade and filled with diverse people, practices, and religions. It was a tremendous challenge for Paul, one he relished as he so loved the people who had come to Christ through his preaching.

When Paul left Corinth, the core principles he taught began to slip away and the Church began to give way to division, unbalanced theology, unorganized worship, and sexual immorality. He touches upon each of these areas in the Corinthian correspondence but, before doing so, he pens some important words early in his first letter, "For I decided to know nothing among you except Jesus Christ, and him crucified" (1 Corinthians 2:2). In other words, Jesus was to be the abiding, drawing, driving, guiding influence. The star of all that was and is Christ.

Reading through the meditations I have offered here, it should come as no surprise that I believe at the heart of God's revelation through the Advent and Christmas story is God's desire to be in a personal relationship with each of his children. God provided an avenue for that relationship through the incarnation. Let us call it the human suit into which God zipped himself in order to come and live among us. God's purpose was to teach, heal, suffer, die, and rise to life again. If we entrust ourselves to God and God's work, we might receive all the benefits of a full and unfettered relationship with God.

When I read the pages of *People*, I encounter those who are still seeking a power beyond themselves to make them feel whole, complete, and maybe even loved. I have been fortunate to have intimate conversations with some people over the years who have, in their time, wielded tremendous fame and power. Whether actor or politician, business mogul or writer, without exception, each would speak of the emptiness of trying to find some meaning in their brief moment on the world's center-stage. And for those who knew and walked with God, they said their faith is where they found ultimate meaning, purpose, and peace.

Some years ago, I read of an interview with Freddie Mercury, the lead singer of the British rock group Queen. He died in 1991. One of the last songs he wrote was "Does Anybody Know What We Are Living For?" Though he was famous, rich, and, in some circles, quite powerful, he confessed in an interview shortly before his death:

> You can have everything in the world and still be the loneliest man, and that is the most bitter type of loneliness. Success has brought me world idolization and millions of pounds, but it's prevented me from having the one thing we all need—a loving, ongoing relationship.[62]

Ah, an ongoing, lasting, enduring relationship. That is what we all need, yes? That is what Christ offers, yes?

Scientists tell us that the light from some of the stars we see could be hundreds, even thousands of years old. You may be looking at a star under your night sky that died eons ago, but the light is still reaching out to you. The light of Christ that began burning brightly some two thousand years ago is still reaching out to you this very moment. But it will never go out. It will never stop reaching out to you. It will never lose its star power. Doubt that? Think on this well-known poem, "One Solitary Life," authored by clergyman James Allen Francis in 1926:

> He was born in an obscure village, the child of a peasant woman. He grew up in still another village, where he worked in a carpenter shop until he was thirty.
>
> Then for three years he was an itinerant preacher. He never wrote a book. He never held an office. He never had a family or owned a house. He didn't go to college. He never visited a big city. He never traveled two hundred miles from the place he was born. He did none

---

62 Nicky Gumble, *Questions of Life* (Colorado Springs: Cook Communications, 2003), 15.

of the things one usually associates with greatness. He had no credentials but Himself.

He was only thirty-three when the tide of popular opinion turned against him. His friends ran away. He was turned over to his enemies. And went through the mockery of a trial.

He was nailed to a cross between two thieves. While he was dying, his executioners gambled for his clothing, the only property he had on Earth. When he was dead, he was laid in a borrowed grave through the pity of a friend.

Twenty centuries have come and gone, and today he is the central figure of the human race and the leader of mankind's progress.

All the armies that ever marched, all the navies that ever sailed, all the parliament that ever sat, all the kings that ever reigned, put together have not affected the life of man on Earth as much as that one solitary life.[63]

Now that is star power. Don't you agree?

— *Preparing Room* —

To what kind of people are you drawn? Why? What qualities of Jesus's life draw you toward him? Why? Have you let his power shine into your heart? If not, why? Why are you waiting to welcome this "one solitary life" as the foundation upon which you can build your life?

---

63 James Allen Francis, *One Solitary Life* (1926).

A Prayer

O Jesus, O Lover of my soul,
Draw from my mind my foolish ambitions and ways,
Draw from my heart my weak fears and anxious
  worries,
Draw from my soul those pockets of want that are
  not from Thee.
Draw me instead unto Thee,
Draw my mind to Thy wisdom and Thy knowledge,
Draw my heart to Thy purity and Thy strength,
Draw my soul to Thy hope and Thy peace.
Draw me O Jesus, Lover of my soul,
Draw me ever more deeply unto Thee,
Draw me to Thy power and might,
And by Thy mercy and grace,
To Thy everlasting life and salvation.
In Your name, this I pray.
Amen.

Gold, Frankenstein, and Mud

On entering the house, they saw the child with
Mary his mother; and they knelt down and paid him
homage. Then opening their treasure chests, they
offered him gifts of gold, frankincense, and myrrh.
And having been warned in a dream not to return
to Herod, they left for their own country by another
road.

—Matthew 2:11–12

As Luke ends his Advent and Christmas telling with shepherds,
Matthew chooses wise men. As I pointed out much earlier in this
book, we have dressed up the story of Jesus's birth. Whenever
the nativity story is shown in celluloid, we see a gathering of all
the players in the story, including the "Three Wise Men." But a
careful reading of scripture clarifies our sanitation. We are never
told there were three and, perhaps more importantly, we see here
that Mary is no longer tending to a baby in a manger. Thank God
she has found a house and it is here that the wise men show up to
pay homage with their gifts.

Somewhere in our history, the architects of Church history gave
the wise men names—Balthazar, Gaspar, and Melchior. The gifts,
however, are detailed in scripture, and they represent the threefold
ministry of Jesus. Gold was given to a king. Frankincense was an
aromatic gum resin used in incense and offered during worship
by a priest. Myrrh was also an aromatic plant resin, but typically
used to anoint a body in preparation for burial. Thus, we see from
early on the foreshadowing of the life of the baby Jesus—king,
priest, and sacrifice.

There is little rest for the poor Holy family in the scene that follows. In order to escape Herod's murderous tirade, they had to divert to Egypt for a season. It all speaks to the kind of roller coaster life that was part of who Jesus came to be from day one. It also tells us of a God, not far away, removed, or on a throne somewhere in a heavenly realm, but one who was willing to come down and live among us. It speaks of a God who literally poured out his life so that each of us could find life by pouring out ourselves to him. Here we see the literal translation of Emmanuel, "God with us"—a word so often associated with this season through which we are traveling.

Some years ago, a clergy friend of mine found himself behind the eight ball in preparing his Christmas Eve sermon. He came home late one evening, frustrated by the days' activities and pressed to get the work done. Failing to greet his family, he entered his study, closed the door, and sat at his desk.

Moments later, one of his children knocked at the door with a quiet whisper. At first, he was irritated and spun around in his chair ready to bark out an order to leave him be. But something inside got hold of him and he welcomed his daughter into his presence.

"Daddy, we want to show you our Christmas play," the young girl said with excitement. It was an in-home production and his four children had been putting together the little play all afternoon. Then, taking her father's hand, she pulled him into the living room where a small card table was set up, covered with a sheet.

Since there were only four children, there was some exchanging of roles, but as they got to the end, his young daughter welcomed her three brothers, each carrying a gift. She said, "And here are the wise men, and they are carrying their gifts. Gold, Frankenstein, and Mud."

My friend did as any loving father would and should have done. He did not say a word about semantics, but clapped and hugged each of his children before getting back to work. He went back into his study and began to think on the little play. He thought of the gifts his children presented, and determined they were not as off center as some might think.

For instance, he knew gold was appropriate, not just for a king, but also because it represented so much of what Jesus taught. Jesus was friend to all. He was friend of the rich, of the poor, and everyone in between. And he spent a good deal of his ministry addressing issues around money and possessions. He was not necessarily a fan of wealth, but was no enemy either. Jesus primarily spoke against indulgence, waste, and greed. Gifts given were to be shared. It is about as simple as that. Yes, gold would play an important role in Jesus's ministry.

Frankenstein was not too far off either. Jesus knew something about how humans could behave like monsters. Through sin and selfishness, the good people God wanted humans to be were often twisted into creatures God would hardly recognize. Covered with scars of anger, gossip, hatred, racism, self-indulgence, violence, and so on, humankind became "Franken-kind." Jesus spent much of his ministry trying to transform those monsters back into the image of God.

Mud represented the dirt of humanity. Jesus knew a good bit about traveling through the filth of the earth. The horror of the Frankensteins he encountered was the living expression of sin which, left unattended, ended in death. Death would have been no stranger to Jesus by the time he reached his young adult years. Jesus also was acquainted with disease, illness, and death. Isaiah prophesied about Jesus:

> He was despised and rejected by others;
> a man of suffering and acquainted with infirmity . . . .
> (Isaiah 53:3)

Jesus spent much of His life healing the physical wounds of the humans he encountered. When it was time to heal their spiritual wounds, death was the chosen path, thus ending his earthly journey and the placement of his body into a rock-hewn tomb. But once he traveled through death, he also chose to defeat it, by rising from it and giving hope to all who might follow him.

So, you can imagine what my friend did. God gave him his Christmas sermon through the innocence of child-inspired wisdom. "Gold, Frankenstein, and Mud." Jesus knew about all three and he knows the struggles you may have with them.

So often our own struggles with wealth, monsters, and filth take us far from the home God wants for us. He promises that he will not leave us or abandon us if we are but willing to take his hand. And when we do, perhaps like the wise men, when our journey has ended we will return to our "own country by another road." Well?

— *Preparing Room* —

Name the struggles you have with your own encounters with gold, Frankenstein, and mud? How can holding Jesus's hand help you through and in those struggles? How can giving your life to Him enable you to return to your "own country"?

A Prayer

We three kings of Orient are,
Bearing gifts we traverse afar,
Field and fountain, Moor and mountain,
Following yonder star.
Born a King on Bethlehem's plain,
gold I bring to crown him again,
King for ever, Ceasing never,
over us all to reign
Frankincense to offer have I:
incense owns a Deity nigh;
prayer and praising, gladly raising,
worship him, God Most High.

Myrrh is mine; its bitter perfume
breathes a life of gathering gloom;
sorrowing, sighing, bleeding, dying,
sealed in the stone-cold tomb.
Glorious now behold him arise,
King and God and Sacrifice;
heaven sings alleluia;
Alleluia, the earth replies.
O star of wonder, star of night,
star with royal beauty bright;
westward leading, still proceeding,
guide us to thy perfect light!

—John Henry Hopkins, d. 1891
From "We Three Kings"[64]

---

64 *The Hymnal*, 128.

Pointing the Way

There was a man sent from God, whose name was John. He came as a witness to testify to the light, so that all might believe through him. He himself was not the light, but he came to testify to the light. The true light, which enlightens everyone, was coming into the world.

—John 1:6–9

As we know, the Gospel of John offers no narrative about the details around Jesus's birth. Perhaps he simply chose to leave that to Jewish scholar Matthew and historian Luke. John instead chooses to paint with a rather broad brushstroke on finding the light—that is, the true light—that enlightens everyone.

For one who makes his living as an institutional church professional, I must remember that Jesus was not overly concerned about the institution of the church. I do not mean that he did not care. We know that he participated in public worship within the synagogue, as was his custom.[65] We also know that he spent time with religious leaders, sometimes asking questions, sometimes teaching, sometimes rebuking. He was not an enemy of religious institutionalism, but his primary goal was to transform lives by healing them and making them whole.

Jesus's first cousin, John the Baptist, says a great deal about what Jesus came to do. John had a rather large following, and a powerful preaching and baptism ministry. However, John's baptism

---

65 Luke 4:16.

was not Christian baptism.[66] His baptism was one of repentance, a symbol of a life that is turning from sin to holiness and of preparation in waiting for the coming Messiah. John's entire vocation was not focused on himself or on religion, but in paving the way for Christ to come.

Soon after Jesus's baptism by John, we see John gently move away from center stage. At the height of his popularity, some thought John, not Jesus, might be the Messiah. When given the chance to take on that role, John stepped aside saying, "I am not the Messiah . . . . He must increase, but I must decrease" (John 3:28, 30).

This must be the prayer of all who want the Christ Child to enter our hearts, lives, and souls. Earlier in this set of meditations, I stated that I have lived my adult life serving the Church as a priest and pastor. I believe that once one enters Christian life, being part of a lively church, a Christ-centered and Spirit-filled community of faith, is essential. But Christ's primary mission was to establish a Kingdom of disciples, not a Kingdom of hierarchy and structure, buildings and policies. John came to help everyone see the way of true peace and salvation. "He must increase, but I must decrease." What does that mean? My mentor and friend John Stott puts it this way:

> Some people become engrossed in the externals of religion. They come to church. They come to be baptized and confirmed. They come to a pastor and seek his counsel. They come to the Bible and read it, together with other religious literature. But it is possible to engage in all these "comings" without ever coming to Jesus Christ himself.[67]

Year after year, I have watched the behavior of what we clergy sometimes call the "C and E Christians"—Christmas and Easter Christians. These are members of the parish or even those who

---

66 Christian baptism was only authorized by Jesus and not until after his death when he commissioned his apostles to baptize in the name of the Father and of the Son and of the Holy Spirit (Matthew 28:19).

67 John Stott, *Why I Am a Christian* (Downer's Grove, IL: InterVarsity Press, 2003), 127.

merely come in off the street for the Advent, Christmas, and Easter "stories." Once or twice a year, they are drawn by the colors, smells, music, and comfort of the story. But then they leave, some not knowing the emptiness that drew them there in the first place, or the promise behind all the pageantry and majesty that can fill that emptiness.

There is so much more to the Advent and Christmas story than meets the eye. Advent—"to come"—is about pointing the way toward the whole meaning of Christmas. Advent says Christmas without Christ is not Christmas at all. John the Baptist did this, perhaps better than anyone, when he said with all humility, "He must increase, but I must decrease." Have you uttered those words?

— *Preparing Room* —

We come now nearly to the end. We have had the opportunity to sweep clean all those things in our heart that may be keeping Christ from His advent— His coming. What other things must be swept away today to help once again in preparing room?

A Prayer

Lord Jesus Christ,
    I am aware that in different ways you have been
    seeking me.
I have heard you knocking at my door.
I believe—
    that your claims are true;
    that you died on the cross for my sins,
    and that you have risen in triumph over death.
Thank you for your loving offer of forgiveness,
    freedom and fulfillment.
Now—

I turn from my sinful self-centeredness.
I come to you as my Savior.
I submit to you as my Lord.
Give me strength to follow you for the rest of my life.
Amen.

—The Reverend Dr. John Stott[68]

---

68 Stott, *Why I Am a Christian*, 132–33.

Afterword: Let Every Heart Prepare Him Room

He was in the world, and the world came into being through him; yet the world did not know him. He came to what was his own, and his own people did not accept him. But to all who received him, who believed in his name, he gave power to become children of God, who were born, not of blood or of the will of the flesh or of the will of man, but of God. And the Word became flesh and lived among us, and we have seen his glory, the glory as of a father's only son, full of grace and truth.

—John 1:10–14

.

If we spend time, as I hope this little book has helped you do, meditating, praying, and reflecting on the Advent and Christmas story, we can quickly see that much of the unfolding of the story depends on how people responded to God's invitations.

It should occur to us that Mary could have said, "No." And though she said "Yes," Joseph could have gone through with his plan to turn her out. And though Joseph said "Yes," Mary's family could have shunned her. And though her family said "Yes" to the babe in her womb, the innkeeper could have said, "No room and no manger. Move along." The wise men could have played Herod's game and brought the whole story to an end, but they said "Yes" to following the star and "Yes" to the child-King. And, of course, when John could have made a run for Jesus's rightful place, he chose to say "Yes" to the Messiah and "No" to the man in the mirror.

As I write this final piece for your consideration, my mother recently ended her battle with cancer by saying "Yes" to whatever gift our heavenly Father offers us after death. I can still remember about a year and a half ago when my father called with the terrible news. The "C" word had, for the first time, entered our immediate family's lives.

For a long eighteen months, my mother said "Yes" to virtually every treatment that came her way, including the constant, consistent, and loving care of my father. "Yes" to medicines, chemotherapy, and radiation. "Yes" to doctors' visits, scans, and x-rays. Even "Yes" to saying goodbye to things that had been part of her daily life—driving, shopping, and vacationing. It is how we cope with life as we watch it dwindle away.

Her heart and the substance of who she was, was being prepared for the next great chapter. Before her last breath, my mother smiled. My faith tells me that was a smile not simply given to those around her, but to the One who was now offering what she was being prepared for throughout her life's journey—more, eternal life. Her life changed; it did not end. Her healing changed; it did not end. The love our family had for her changed; it did not end. At the end, she received yet another miracle: the end of death is the beginning of life.

As I believe my dear mother knew, in order to experience all of the life, love, and healing God wants for all of us, there is the acceptance of his invitation. Our God is a loving God. He will not force himself upon us. He comes with that good word to each of us, "Greetings, favored one." What follows is a promise of all the things any human soul could ever want, both here and in the life beyond.

In many of the churches I have served, there are little cards in the back of the pews where visitors can ask to be called upon, members can offer prayer requests, and children can scribble drawings. I have kept a few of them throughout the years. One of the cards in the offering plate made its way to my desk that next Monday morning. Obviously, a child had written the words, "Dear God, I love you a lot. I wish that I could meet you in person."

The birth of Jesus gives us each a chance to not just read about Jesus, but to meet him in person. I wonder if the clutter, now moved from your heart, has prepared room for him to take up residence in a new way that perhaps he has not done before. Maybe the old anger you have been holding onto is now gone, and it can be replaced with charity. Maybe fear has been brushed away, and faith can now take its place. Perhaps grief and sadness have too long been your companions, and now there is room for joy and laughter. Maybe addiction or sin has been released and now there is recovery and forgiveness. Now maybe loneliness and isolation will finally be met with companionship and salvation.

It is a matter of saying "Yes" to God's invitation. The story we have lived through these days together is a reminder that we are not alone and we are not without resources to face whatever comes our way.

Throughout my adult life, one of my real heroines has been Corrie Ten Boom. She was a wonderful Dutch Christian who survived the Ravensbrück Concentration Camp during World War II and went on to become one of the leading evangelists and missionaries of the twentieth century. She used to tell the story of an encounter she had with a young student named Anton, who attended one of her Bible classes in Holland. Anton was severely mentally challenged and he could neither speak nor walk alone. He was in Corrie's class for a short time.

> Anton listened to my Bible stories, but when I spoke too long to suit him, he yawned . . . I did not know how much Anton really understood.
>
> Once I took his hand and touched his five fingers one after another and said, "Jesus loves Anton so much."
>
> The next week, when Anton saw me, he took my hand and with his fingers outspread, looked at me with a face full of longing.
>
> "Jesus loves Anton so much," I repeated, touching a finger at every word. Then I taught him to do it himself.
>
> After that, every week, Anton showed me with his fingers how much Jesus loved him.

The last time I saw him, I told him while he touched his fingers with his right hand, "Jesus loves Anton so much. How thankful I am for that! You too, Anton?"

"Yes," Anton said, as his face lit up.

It was the only word I ever heard from Anton . . . it is the most worthwhile word that any person can speak to the Lord Jesus.[69]

"In the beginning was the Word and the Word was with God and the Word was God." God has been whispering since the dawn of time, "I love you so much." Advent and Christmas whisper, "I love you so much." And now, even as you read these pages, God whispers, "I love you so much."

What do we do with God's offer? What do we do with God's invitation? We can certainly reject it. God has left that choice to us and even that comes out of love. But far better it is to simply say "Yes," and do so by preparing room.

A Prayer
Joy to the world!
The Lord is come:
Let earth receive her King;
Let every heart prepare him room . . .[70]
And your heart . . .
And my heart . . .
Prepare Him room . . .
Amen.

---

69 Corrie Ten Boom, *Clippings from My Notebook* (Minneapolis: World Wide Publications, 1982). 120–21. By permission of SPCK.

70 *The Hymnal*, 100.

Acknowledgments

And now, some words of thanks.

I once read these words of biblical commentator George M. Adams, "Encouragement is oxygen to the soul." I am grateful for a circle of encouragers who have made this work, and my writing ministry, come to life.

First, and foremost, my wife of over thirty-five years, Laura; and my three children, Evie, Jones, and Luke.

Next, I hold deep gratitude for those women listed on the dedication page, some of whom are still on this side of the veil of life, and others who have begun life anew—each serving as "God bearers" in my own spiritual journey—helping me to understand just a bit more, though no doubt tremendous deficiencies remain, a feminine view of God's story to us.

To those who carefully read this book and offered their endorsements—each of whom remain good friends and mentors—The Very Reverend Ian Markham, Ms. Lani Netter, Dr. Neal Berte, and Ann Claypool Beard.

To the wonderful "family" of encouragers with Church Publishing, Nancy Bryan, Ryan Masteller, and Milton Brasher-Cunningham, who carefully worked with me, sifted, edited, and congealed in ways that made my words more accessible to you, my readers.

To my Doctoral Advisor and first publisher, The Reverend Dr. Fisher Humphreys with *Insight Press*.

To my colleagues, and friends, at St. Martin's—our Communications Department Sue Davis, David Bolin, and Aleeta Bureau; to the Rector's staff—Lesley Hough, Carol Gallion, Brittney Jacobson, Allie Hippard and all the members of St. Martin's who allow, and help me, guard and protect my schedule for projects like this one.

And finally, and most importantly of course, to the God of us all, who gives us His grace, love, words, and salvation not just for a season, but for all of time; in the face, life, and name of His son Jesus—Emmanuel—God with us.

Scriptural Index

Genesis

1:2 38
1:26 ix
16:7 87
2:7 3
3:5 49
22:11 87
26:24 19

Exodus

23:20 87

Deuteronomy

1:21 19
1:29 19

Joshua

2:6 3

Judges

6:22 87

Ruth

4:18–22 2

2 Samuel

7:16 33
12 3

1 Kings

19:7 87

1 Chronicles

3:10–17 2

Psalms

23:4 22
51 48
89:3 33
103:12 47

Ecclesiastes

3:1 57
3:5 57

Isaiah

7:14 52
9:7 33
53:3 112

Jeremiah

33:17 33

Daniel

2:44 33
6:26–27a 13
8:16–26 14
9:20–27 14

Hosea

12:4 87

Jonah

1:10 76
1:17 76
2:1 76

Micah

4:7 33
5:2 97

Habakkuk

2:4 77

Matthew

1:1–17 2
1:5 3
1:6–7 3
1:18 38
1:19 41
1:20 45
1:21 49
1:22–23 52
1:24 45
1:25 55
2:11–12 110
2:13 87
2:1–6 97
2:16–23 102
2:7–8 101
2:9–10 105
4:17 91
6:13 102
7:1–2 35
26:28 15
28:19 116
28:20 39

Mark

7:21 102
7:30 102
9:24 77
14:24 15

Luke

1:1–4 6
1:5–25 60
1:11–20 14
1:26–27 10

1:28 14
1:29 18
1:30 21
1:31a 24
1:31b 28
1:32–33 32
1:34 35
1:35 38
1:36–37 59
1:38 64
1:39–45 67
1:46–56 71
1:57–66 62
2:1–6 75
2:7 .... 79, 83
2:8–11 86
2:12–25 89
2:16–20 93
3:1–22 62
3:23–28 2
4:16 115
22:20 15
22:43 87
23:42 51

John

1:1–5 ix
1:6–9 115
1:10–14 119
3:3 15
3:20 102
3:28 116
10:24–25 87
13:34 15
14:27 19
16:5–16 39
3:30 116

Acts

2:1–13 39
12:7 87

Romans

1:17 77
3:23 43
12:9 102

1 Corinthians

2:2 106
12:9 77

2 Corinthians

3:17 99

Galatians

3:26–28 4
5:22 77

Hebrews

11:31 3
13:5 94
2:7 87

James

2:25 3

1 John

4:18 22

Jude

6 87

Index of Authors Cited

Aelred of Rievaulx, *92*

Austen, Jane, *66*

Boethius, *17*

Boom, Corrie Ten, *40, 122*

Book of Common Prayer, The, 104

Burns, Robert, *10*

Columbanus, *34*

Counsell, Michael, *17, 20, 27, 37, 44, 58, 66, 100*

Cranmer, Thomas, *58*

De Lima, Sister Rose, *92*

Francis, James Allen, *108*

Gumble, Nicky, *107*

Hamman, Adalbert G., *63*

Hays, Edward, *33*

Hopkins, John Henry, *114*

Hymnal, The, xi, 83, 114, 122

Iswolsky, Helen, *82*

John of Kronstadt, *44*

Larson, Craig Brian, *26*

Lewis, C. S., *57*

Luther, Martin, *85*

Rowell, Edward K., *77*

Stevenson, Robert Louis, *20*

Stott, John, *51, 116, 118*

Taylor, Jeremy, *100*

Temple, William, *37*

Tutu, Desmond, *73*

Tutu, Mpho, *73*

Tychon of Zadonsk, *82*

Van de Weyer, Robert, *34*

Yin-liu, Ernest Yang, *27*

Zahn, Andrew, *26*

Explore more books in the series

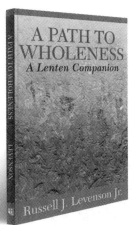

9781640653177

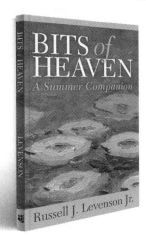

9781640652712

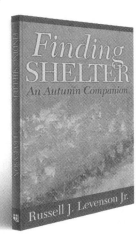

9781640652699

CHURCH PUBLISHING INCORPORATED

Church Publishing products can be ordered by calling **(800)-242-1918,** online at **churchpublishing.org,** or through any Episcopal, religious, secular bookstore, or through any online bookseller.